FIND YOUR MIND

# FIND YOUR MIND

MEDITATION FOR THE BOLD
AND AMBITITOUS

ANDREW FEINSTEIN

NEW DEGREE PRESS

COPYRIGHT © 2018 ANDREW FEINSTEIN

FIND YOUR MIND

*Meditation for the Bold and Ambitious*

ISBN     978-1-64137-175-9  *Paperback*

978-1-64137-176-6  *Ebook*

*To all of those who have helped me, all of those who have hurt me and all those I have yet to meet. To any person on my journey, this book is for you.*

# CONTENTS

# PREFACE

---

*"It's dark in here, I am scared."*

*"I have no idea where I am."*

*"There's a sound like breathing; deep breathing."*

*"It's haunting; almost as if it is me breathing... that is how close it feels."*

*"Should I be able to feel my heart beat like this? It is pounding on my chest. It feels like it is going to explode any second busting out of my chest and landing in my hands."*

*"Where am I? How did I get here? What is the last thing I remember?"*

*"Nothing, I remember nothing."*

*"It's dark in here, I am scared."*

— ANDREW'S MIND DIARY, ENTRY 1

*"I can't move."*

*"Even when I try, I simply can't do it."*

*"What is happening to me? Where did I go wrong?"*

*"All I can feel is pain. It is not sharp or piecing, it doesn't ache, it is a subtle pain. It is as if I know that the real stuff is coming."*

*"I give up!"*

*"Whoever, whatever is doing this to me, I give up."*

*"You win."*

— ANDREW'S MIND DIARY, ENTRY 2

*"I can feel the pain intensifying, starting in my heart and slowly spreading through my veins."*

*"I want it to be over, I want it to stop."*

*"It has been weeks since I started living in darkness, trapped with no way out."*

*"I keep trying to feel around for objects, trying to find anything to help me."*

*"But, there is nothing."*

*"No food, no water, no warmth, no light... just darkness, despair and crippling loneliness."*

*"No one is coming for me."*

*"I remember thinking this day one, but now I really know; I am alone."*

*"Only thing to do is wait. To shut my eyes and wait...for a savior or for deaths cold embrace."*

— ANDREW'S MIND DIARY, ENTRY 3

*"My eyes have been closed for what feels like months, but death has not yet come"*

*"I am unsure how I am still alive."*

*"There is nothing here, no sounds, no feelings, nothing other than my breath."*

*"Wait a minute, that breathing I heard first, it was mine..."*

*"Maybe I have just been haunting myself...I am confused, I need to just clear my head."*

*"I cannot focus, not with the sound of this breathing."*

*"Why fight it when you can listen to it?" a voice said from off the distance.*

*"Who the hell was that? Who are you? Show yourself!"*

*"There is no one there...maybe I am imagining things, maybe I am going crazy"*

*"Or maybe I should just listen."*

— ANDREW'S MIND DIARY, ENTRY 4

*"It has been two days since I starting listening to my breath."*

*"It is all I do."*

*"Inhaling, I feel the air enter my lungs filling my entire being with life."*

*"Exhaling, I feel my energy released, vacating my body to join the world."*

*"Nothing has changed, but I feel much better... I feel content. Even with the darkness, I feel like I have found meaning, purpose. There is a harmony that comes from watching my breath. I can feel the forces of inhale and exhale working with one another, keeping me alive."*

*"I think I may have found why I am here."*

*"I think the reason for being alive may be found within."*

— ANDREW'S MIND DIARY, ENTRY 5

*"I have stopped looking externally."*

*"The answers I seek, they can all be found within me."*

*"If I can observe, knowledge, wisdom, hope, love, meaning, will all be revealed to me."*

*"My life has meaning, not because it changed, but because I changed how I look at it."*

*"There it is."*

*"I can see it."*

*"The light, my light."*

—ANDREW'S MIND DIARY, ENTRY 6

# INTRODUCTION

---

Meditation has a branding problem.

Many individuals would cultivate images of monks practicing in isolated caves or hippies sitting with their eyes closed chanting the word "om" repeatedly. We all have an idea of what we think meditation looks like and this idea often keeps us away. However, the image we have of meditation is not the reality.

Over the past year, I have studied, researched, and interviewed more than 100 of the world's top, young, performers, athletes, and business people who use meditation and mindfulness. Through their stories and my own experience, I want to show you that meditation is a practice, a practice that allows you to embrace the present moment. Meditation is something from which we can all benefit.

**

It was as if I was standing on a carpet that was pulled from underneath me to reveal a glass floor showing the huge drop to the ground below. I felt like I was barely able to hang on and maybe any minute that the glass would crack and I would fall to my ultimate demise.

College was the first time in my very young life that I felt completely unbalanced.

Everyone had told me it would be the best four years of my life.

However, college was not the joy-filled experience promised on all the college blogs, tours, and websites. Rather it was a nightmare that had enough plot twists to drive any horror movie fan crazy.

I remember the crippling loneliness, the feelings of meaninglessness, the worry that I didn't belong, that I didn't matter to anyone. I remember coming home the first few nights of freshman year and crying into my pillow. I remember drinking just to numb the pain. I remember wanting to transfer, drop out, go home, do anything to get out of this place.

And my journey was probably easier than many.

Suicide and depression are at an all-time high in our country, with suicide being the second leading cause of deaths among people age 15–34.[1] According to the 2018 American College Health Association survey, 40% of college students report feeling "so depressed that it was difficult to function."[2] The American Disability Association says there are ~40 million people who suffer from an anxiety disorder and 75% of them experience their first episode of anxiety before the age of 22.[3]

For many, college is the first time where young people begin to grapple with issues regarding the future, who and what they want to be. Before this life was simple, doing what you were told with no preoccupation with what came next. However, with internal struggles like making new friends, leaving home, job prospects and more, college students are heavily prone to depression.

---

1   "Suicide". 2018. *National Institute Of Mental Health.*
2   Baker, K. 2014. "How Colleges Flunk Mental Health." *Newsweek.*
3   "Mental Health and College Students." *Anxiety and Depression Association of America.*

Furthermore, only 1 in 8 college students consider themselves to be thriving or truly enjoying his or her time. What does this mean? Well first, college is not the carefree bundle of joy that everyone sells it as, and second, there must be a larger problem as graduates continue to peddle the same narrative of fun, friends, and future that rarely meets expectations.

Now I am not trying to bash college into the ground, because frankly I came away from my experience thinking highly of my alma mater and feeling as if it helped me become the best version of myself. But there was no guidebook or quick hack to the first few years that chewed me up and spit me back out. Unfortunately, I do not have a solution. Everyone's journey is individual and every person finds himself or herself when they are ready. That said, I am here to explain why this book is imperative for the college audience and why I could not wait to write it.

**

As a looked down at the figurative glass floor below my feet, I was terrified of falling. I was terrified that I wouldn't make it through college that the pressure would overwhelm me and I would figuratively fall, plummeting to my utter failure.

Instead, I found meditation, my harness. Meditation became a technique and a practice that I could fall back on when things got tough, when I failed a test or had my heart broken or felt like I had no clue what I wanted to do with my life. Every time my glass floor started to crack, I no longer needed to worry for I had meditation holding me securely.

Meditation, for me, is a tool that allows me to live in the present moment while also helping let go of things that get in the way of the former. By focusing on the breath, I can situate in the here and now, noticing everything that is going on in the present while simultaneously letting distractions fade away.

Meditation is a not just a method reserved for monks, it is a powerful tool that allows us to be happier, helping provide more value to our lives.

I don't claim to be an expert in meditation — I reserve that for a very select group of individuals in this world like the Dalai Lama — but I am invested and active in teaching and spreading meditation. I'm still learning daily — but I do know this, there is something powerful about meditation. Unfortunately, there are not enough people teaching and sharing insights for us, the bold and ambitious.

So here I am.

This book will offer you a customized roadmap and playbook to find your own path to make meditation part of your life.

Meditation does indeed have a branding problem.

Superman probably meditates.

You probably should too.

Here's how – for people like you and me.

# MAPPING YOUR JOURNEY

———

Think of this book like a travel agent, you tell it where you want to go and it will show you how to get there. Here are some tricks for getting the most out of your "travel agent."

## YOU

This book starts with you. Meditation, though found in many traditions, is an individual journey. Yes, you might have a community that you sit with and a tradition you pull from, but no one can meditate for you, no one can breathe for you, no one can live your life for you. Ultimately, only you can decide how much you get out of this book.

Before you embark on this journey, I want you to think about one question:

**Everyone's life is on a path: where is yours heading?**

What do you see in your future, how do you want to live your life, how do you want to better yourself, how do you want to use this book?

This book is not just about meditation; it is a guide, a how-to book on bettering your life made just for you. My goal is for you to come away from this book feeling happier and knowing that there is a practice out there waiting for YOU.

## WHERE TO START?

This book is comprised of four sections: Setting the Scene, Learning a Lot, Role Meditators, Jump-Starting Your Journey. The beginning sets the stage for why meditation is so important, showing you the why before we get into the what. From here, the layout assumes you are starting with no meditation experience and culminates with the hope that you will feel comfortable starting a practice or at least learning how meditation can best serve you. The structure is meant to serve as a guide. You, however, know yourself better than I do so my guidance can only provide so much.

Each person is at a different point in their life journey. You may have never heard of meditation, or you may be an avid practitioner who knows much more than I do. Maybe, you are skeptical or adverse to the idea of meditation. Maybe you are curious but just haven't learned enough yet. Wherever you are on your journey, whether it is building on what you already know or setting a foundation for you to return to one day, I think there is something this book offers.

Regardless of where you are on your journey, it is always beneficial to look at yourself as a beginner. In an endless world of knowledge, there is always more to learn. So, even if you are an expert, I recommend you still read through the first few chapters on the basic information, because who knows, it might solicit some new information, or at the very least reinforce everything you already know to be true. Beyond that, here are some guidelines to help YOU read this book:

- **FNP (Friendly New Person)**: Someone who has never experienced meditation before. For you I recommend paying close attention to the beginning of this book: "Setting the Scene." It will be important to learn why and how meditation will work for you. This will take some reflection and understanding of the concepts that I present in this section. Beyond that, I recommend doing the exercises as they come up throughout the book and just experiment. Try to learn as much as you can.

It might be helpful to read a little bit at a time, as all of this information can be overwhelming.

- **Novice**: You have tried meditation a few times, but are still confused about what this thing is. I would read through the beginning material: "Setting the Scene". However the real value for you is in "Learning a Lot". You want to get a really good feel for what practices you think will work best for you. Definitely try to do some exercises along the way and just experiment with all of this material.

- **Seasoned Beginner**: You have been meditating for a few years now, being pretty consistent in your practice. The beginning material: "Setting the Scene" and "Learning a Lot," might be worth skimming, but the real magic for you is going to be in the latter half of the book: "Role Meditators" and "Jump Starting Your Journey". This section will explain how best to build a more consistent practice and one that is perfect for you.

- **Semi-Professional**: You have a solid daily practice with an intrigue in meditation, maybe you have even gone on a few retreats. For you I would recommend that you skim the first few chapters to see if my ideas align with your practice. I would then read the "Role Meditators." See if there is anyone in here that interests you, you might find someone that you would want to learn more about. I would also give some attention to the section "Jump Starting Your Journey" for you might find new practices and tips to augment what you do currently.

- **His Holiness the Dalai Lama**: His Holiness if you are reading this I am truly honored! If you consider yourself to be a practitioner of this caliber, then I recommend you read whatever title jumps out at you. I think that there is always value in hearing something explained in a new light, from a new voice. You might just learn something new.

## THIS IS JUST A BOOK

I think books are incredible. I think that they provide so much knowledge and power and serve such an amazing purpose. However, at the end of the day our lives are more than just books.

That is why I am looking to provide more than that. This book is supposed to be a teaser, almost like those motivational videos you see on Facebook or YouTube that make you want to go out and effect change in your life.

That is what I want to do with this book. I want to inspire you to make an impact on both yourself and the world.

I recently crossed a book off my long reading list, *Man's Search for Meaning* by Victor Frankel, a non-fiction novel that details a first-hand account of the Holocaust and provides an argument for how Frankel and others managed to survive these circumstances both physically and psychologically. One of the many things that stood out to me was a passage in the foreword of the book. It said, "Typically, if a book has one passage, one idea with the power to change a person's life, that alone justifies reading, it rereading it, and finding room for it on one's shelf." Frankel's book has several such passages.

This is an idea that I embodied when writing the book you are about to read. I hope that even one passage, one sentence, one word in this book, will change your life. If and when you find that passage, I want you to put it back on your shelf and make that change.

At the end of the day, this is just a book.

**Your life** that is where the real magic is.

# PART I

## SETTING THE SCENE

*"Thousands of candles can be lighted from a single candle, and the life of the candle will not be shortened. Happiness never decreases by being shared."*

— BUDDHA

# CHAPTER 1

# THE CURSE OF THE MEDITATION GENERATION

———

What is your favorite birthday that you can remember?

Mine is my fourth birthday. Yes, I can remember it. Plus, even if I couldn't there is video evidence of the happiness I experienced. I remember that my mom got a magician by the name of Magic Al to perform for all of my friends and me.

Magic Al called me, the birthday boy, up to the stage and had me show the audience how to use one of those fake boxing gloves attached to an extending arm. He then proceeded to pretend that I was hitting him with the glove as I would extend it and he would let it hit him in the face.

When I tell you that I have never laughed like that... It was hands down the funniest thing to me at the time. It was the first time in my life that my stomach hurt from laughing so hard.

As I sit here recounting this story, thinking about my over-sized white button down with blue flowers, picturing my mom's short hair and red lipstick, remembering the smells of freshly cut grass in the backyard, it is hard to believe that that was 18 years ago. How can a memory so vivid be so far away?

I can remember the first day I went to school, the first person I ever had a crush on, the first time I failed a quiz, the first time I fell in love, all these memories in my head as if they are a movie. All of these experiences brought me here and made me the person that I am right now.

Crazy to think that just a few years ago I was a kid, now I am an adult with a 401k, who is worried about paying bills, keeping a job, getting married – that is barely of fraction of my list.

## LIVING LIFE ON AUTOPILOT

150 mph – that is how most of us live our lives.

We are always running and as cliché as it may sound, most of us never stop and smell the roses.

Well, I did.

Yeah, I actually stopped the other day to take a moment to smell the roses, and personally, I prefer the smell of a bustling coffee shop, but I understand the metaphor. We always want to be doing the next thing, constantly moving towards some greater goal, a goal that we cannot even see.

This pattern starts at such an early age as middle schoolers often start concerning themselves with which college they should attend. They worry about what classes to take, what sports to play, what charities to support. They start scheduling all this time, building up a resume, but rarely do they just enjoy the moment, rather they are just working their way to the next goal: college.

Then in college, we start thinking about our first job. At that job, we try to find our path to the top. Then when we get to the top we are so confused because we don't know where to go next, we don't know how to just be present in this moment.

We reach our goals but our celebration is short-lived. We end up setting a new goal, always striving for more, on a journey that never ends and leads to perpetual dissatisfaction.

Now I am unsure where this journey starts within us, where we get this constant need of striving for more. However, I know for sure that this journey eventually ends and that ending for all human beings is death. Now while this may seem morbid on the surface, it is really a cry of hope rather than one of tragedy. It shows us the reality of our existence, and this recognition gives us the opportunity to change it.

**

Mariann Johnson is a Mindfulness Facilitator and Implementation Manager at Moment Health, United Health Group. In her role, she leads corporate mindfulness retreats, with the goal of helping employees take a step back from the stressful work environment and hopefully better their work ethic and demeanor. She told me a story of an upper-level corporate employee who for the sake of this recount will be named Jim.

Jim's company signed the entire staff up for one of these retreats, the plan being to head into the rural country of Wisconsin for a weekend getaway of meditation and deep personal insight. Jim did not really want to attend this retreat, feeling that it would be a waste of time, a pointless excursion aimed at unsuccessfully building employee morale. He felt that his time would be better spent anywhere else.

After the night of scheduled programming ranging from structured meditations and talks to personal evaluation, the retreat staff urged the employees to return to their rooms and enjoy the peace and quiet of the silent evening. Jim, however, found himself called to sit on the dock by the lake and simply stare at the stars.

"I do not know how long I was out there, but as I sat and just observed, I started to think what else in my life I could have missed," Jim told the retreat staff the following morning.

He finally took a step back from the forward inertia of his life to realize all of the things he was missing. Had he missed his own personal growth? Or his kids growing up? Was he ever truly present? These questions started to creep up as he sat staring at one of nature's beautiful gifts.

Jim started his meditation practice the very next day.

This story illustrates the way in which most of us live our lives, we are always looking for the next thing, unable to sit in the present moment and truly soak up all that life has to offer. Jim's story shows the ability of every individual to take a step back, to look up at the stars, or smell the roses. To witness all that life has to offer. Jim started meditating so that he could stop running on autopilot so that he could try and practice being in the present moment in hopes of making it a habit in his life. Rather than get defeated and feel like he had wasted so much time, Jim used his experience as an opportunity to make a change.

Instead of driving full speed ahead, why can't we take our foot off the gas every once in a while and see all that life has to offer, truly enjoying the experience of being alive, rather than rushing to get somewhere else.

## WHY ARE YOU HERE?

So, why are you here? Why did you buy this book? I am sure that the answers may vary, but ultimately you all bought this book for the same reason. It is even the reason why I wrote the book. **Happiness.** If we boil down our reasoning for everything that we do, happiness is always the answer. It is the pot of gold at the end of the rainbow, and it is what we are striving for constantly. Yet, despite our desire for it, we rarely find happiness, and when we do, we struggle to hold onto it. Even worse, sometimes we are happy and don't even recognize what we have until we experience the other side of the coin, suffering.

Even though we are constantly striving for happiness, no one ever defines it for us. If I asked you to define happiness right now, you would probably look at me as if I were crazy.

"Come on Andrew, everyone knows what happiness is."

Then you might realize no one has ever asked you to define this word. So when I push for an answer you might try to make something up but often it will seem like it doesn't encompass the true meaning of happiness. Contemplating this phenomenon, I remember trying to define happiness myself.

A dictionary definition told me that happiness was the state of being happy, which helps no one. So I clicked on happy and the results came back as being in a state of content or pleasure. Immediately I thought of something that gives me pleasure, junk food.

I love sweets, I try not to eat them often, but I love them. And looking at our Webster dictionary, we can assume that in order for me to be as happy as possible, I need to eat as much junk food as I possibly can. Well I tried this and after about half a tub of Ben &Jerry's Fish Food in... Okay I am lying: it was two tubs of Ben &Jerry's, a brownie, a piece of cake, some kettle corn, and a handful or two of Swedish fish. After this experience, I found myself as unhappy as

I had been in a while. My stomach felt like it was going to explode, and I could barely move. This wasn't happiness, this was a food coma!

After this experience, I set out to try and figure out what happiness actually is. I talked to others seeing if they had similar experiences and found overwhelming agreement with many of the feelings that I was having. We hold happiness as this sacred object we are all striving for, yet we don't know where to find it, how to find it, or what to do with it once we do find it.

So, take a minute to pause and reflect on your own life, can you think of a time where you were truly happy? Do not search too hard, just see what pops into your mind right away.

For me, my mind immediately goes to a vision of myself, alone, behind the steering wheel of my Jeep, blasting music with the windows down on a beautiful sunny day and just belting out the words to the song at the top of my lungs. Or the feeling of belly laughing about nonsense with a loved one. Or the smell of coffee on a really lazy morning. Everyone has a different answer, but there is something underlying all of these examples. This led me to the basis for my definition of happiness.

**Happiness is a state of living in the present moment, free of concern.**

When we are truly present in what we are doing and we are not worried about what has happened in the past of what will happen in the future, we can experience true happiness, lasting happiness.

When I started to do this ethnographic research, asking people to recount a happy moment, I assumed that everyone would give examples of big milestones in their lives, like graduation or getting some huge award, getting married or witnessing the birth of one's child, but not once did someone bring this up. We might look back and remember those experiences as being important, but they are often stressful and we struggle to be present in these moments. Instead, I found the same answers as mine from above, that happiness was found in the little moments, the times when we felt like we were truly present.

Happiness, however, is a two-sided coin. One side is happiness and the other is suffering. Yes, suffering, a state all too familiar in our world. But, even with this sentiment, there is beauty in our suffering, for without suffering we would have no understanding of happiness, life would simply be an 80 year long monotone speech.

Suffering is prevalent often more than happiness as a decrease in happiness is a quantifiable amount of suffering. But suffering is not nearly as daunting as it may appear.

That being said, I want you to think about a time when you suffered. Just like our happiness exercise, don't think too hard, just use the first thing that came to mind. This example may bring up difficult feelings and emotions, but simply try and see the situation, try and understand what was happening both externally and internally.

No two people will have the exact same situation in mind, this is impossible, but it is possible to find the underlying connection behind human suffering.

**Suffering is simply attachment.**

It is the desire to cling to previous states of mind or attach ourselves to future aspirations. Suffering takes us out of the present moment and places an unnecessary stress on obtaining something that we do not have in this moment.

Let's look at the example of going to the gym. Often times we go to the gym in order to look a certain way, we get attached to a certain body image and we lock in on achieving that goal. This can get in the way of us being able to truly enjoy the exercise and bathe in the endorphins released from a blood-pumping workout. Rather we are annoyed that we have not hit our ideal physique and we beat ourselves up claiming that we didn't work hard enough.

What if we just enjoyed being in the gym and getting a good workout in, letting go of our desires to be somewhere other than right here, right now. We would not only be happy but we would also be getting in better shape along the way. We can choose to cling to certain things and let that distract us from life or we can try and be present and truly enjoy everything life has to offer.

I am sure you might be thinking, "This is a book on meditation, where does meditation come into all of this talk about happiness and suffering?"

**Meditation is a tool that allows one to place oneself in the present moment, and when thoughts and distractions arise, meditation teaches one to notice them but not attach, to let these thoughts pass.**

So, honestly, meditation fits right in the middle being a practice that can create happiness and teach us how to deal with our suffering.

We all remember high school math and logical proofs (A leads to B, B leads to C, so A leads to C). Well following a logical argument, one can make the case that meditation leads to happiness.

- (A) Meditation
- (B) The Present Moment
- (C) Happiness

Meditation is a tool to situate yourself in the present moment (A → B). When we are living in the present moment we are happy (B → C) Therefore, meditation can make us happier (A → C).

On the other side of the coin, meditation can help us find comfort in our suffering, helping us practice letting go of attachments. When distracting thoughts start to arise, we can simply learn to let them go, shifting back to the breath and the present.

So you see; meditation is the perfect tool. It is a tool that can truly help you live your best life. You just need to use it.

## THIS IS THE MEDITATION GENERATION

When you are a kid all you want to do is grow up but when you get there you realize that every once in a while, it would be so great to be a kid again. I mean imagine how well you would do in first grade with all the knowledge you have now, plus don't forget about nap time.

As a kid, we cannot wait to grow up, to be done with school and homework, to be able to work a job and live on our own. However, becoming a grown-up is not all its cracked up to be. High school, college, post-graduation, the period from ages 15 to 30 is no easy time in our lives. It is a period of continuous change and new stages of life, new friends, new family maybe. It is a time where things become well more complicated. We have to start worrying about college, then our career, then our family, then our retirement. We worry about fitting in and finding meaning, having a voice and being heard. It is crazy how much there is to be worried about these days. I mean I thought it was bad enough when I had to worry about studying for my spelling test, now if you spell something wrong in an email it could be the difference as to whether you get the job you are applying for.

Clearly, the brochure to becoming an adult forgets to mention all of the hardships that come with the transition.

Isolation, loneliness, meaningless – these three have been the hardest for me to deal with as I have started to become a self-serving individual.

Isolation – being left to my own thoughts. When I feel isolated, I feel like I am cornered off, trapped in my world, a world of self-doubt and sabotage. A cruel world where I will never be happy.

Loneliness – feeling alone even when people are around. This is feeling like no one understands me, as if I am invisible. It goes beyond isolation because it makes me feel like I will never have anyone. It feels as though I will always be alone.

Meaninglessness – feeling like I do not belong anywhere. It is feeling like I do not matter, not just to other people, but also to myself. It is as if I could disappear and no one would notice. It is a feeling that no matter how hard I try I will always be a failure.

These states of mind have hurt me the most. Not only have I struggled to deal with these states, I also, for the longest time, I was unable to articulate them, outsourcing my feelings to more tangible pains like relationship issues or lack of social events. For example, when a party would occur and I was not on the list, I would get angry at the hosts, rather than embrace the isolation I felt underneath.

Instead of trying to go inside and understand these feelings, I, and many of my fellow humans, try to cover them up with drinking, drugs, sex, social media, Netflix and anything else we can find. We desperately try to attach to anything that will keep us on the surface, terrified of what may be lurking below. Our generation wants to remain surface level, because lying underneath is a truth that is too hard to face. The truth is we all feel meaningless at times. We all have moments when it feels like no one cares about us, and no matter what we do, we will never be good enough.

This book tries to show that we are good enough, that there is meaning in everything that we do. If we can sit and embrace the present for what it is, we can start to find an understanding for our feelings. If we can embrace our feelings, we can understand them, if we can understand them, we can overcome them. This is not an easy task, and it can be scary at times to try to accept the deeper feelings within you, but it is always worth it. Life is too short to avoid what is real, so let us embrace it—together.

Yael Shy, author of *What Now? Meditation for your Twenties and Beyond*, believes that this is the meditation generation. In her work at New York University, she is starting to see a huge increase in popularity for meditation.

"When I first started working here, only a few people would show up for meditations, most of whom had never had any prior experience," Yael told me. "Now we will see something like 500 students showing up all of whom know something about meditation. So something is changing."

We as a people need something to counteract the era where everything seems to be fake, where social media shows only the happy fragments of people's lives and it is even hard to know which news is real. We need something to help us understand this lack of meaning and purpose. We need something to help us not feel so alone and isolated. We need something real.

Meditation allows us to touch something that is real, something that can teach us and show us that being real, being present that is where life's beauty lies.

We are the meditation generation.

We just need to prove it.

CHAPTER 2

# WHAT IS MEDITATION ANYWAY?

———

*When your attention moves into the Now, there is an alertness. It is as if you were waking up from a dream, the dream of thought, the dream of past and future. Such clarity, such simplicity. No room for problem-making. Just this moment as it is."*

— ECKHART TOLLE

**

I want to preface this section by saying that my knowledge of meditation is not complete – I am still learning daily. I am, however, a big supporter who wants to add to the conversation. With that in mind, I will try and be very careful with the language that I use, as often there are very specific types and variations of meditation and I don't want it to seem like I am using any form contrary to its definition.

So what do I mean when I say I meditate every morning and evening?

For me, this means anywhere from 5–30 minutes of breath focus, of paying attention to my breathing in the present moment. The general goal of my meditation is deeper acceptance of and insight into myself as I am right now. For me, the best way I have found to do this is by using my breath to anchor to the present moment, watching the breath enter and leave my body as if I were an outside observer.

This isn't the exact definition of meditation or the perfect way to do it.

Frankly, meditation comes in a lot of flavors and varieties. Different traditions will adapt and mold the bigger idea of Meditation (uppercase M) in different ways, stressing specific meditation (lowercase m) techniques. These can range from visualization techniques, to sound-healing classes and sensory deprivation baths. Meditation is not one-size-fits-all, which means that as an individual, you need to decide what exercises and methods work best for you. But luckily you do not need to discover these methods for yourself you can borrow them from the general collective; that is why I describe this journey as being both individual and collective.

When I share meditation, I give very little guidance. My belief is that every person, including you, has his or her own innate capacity to meditate and my providing a laundry list of guidelines only impedes the journey. If I asked you to meditate right now, I am sure you would have some mental association with the practice providing a general guideline for how to participate. For instance, if I sat down in front of you, closing my eyes and sitting still, you would most likely mimic my actions.

You ay feel like you are doing it incorrectly, but when you start with what you know, we can build from that. This is much better than setting up a strict definition that makes you feel like you are failing. I simply will try to give a little outline on the form, almost as if I were a personal trainer helping you start working out. Just enough guidance so you feel comfortable doing the practice but still providing enough freedom to find what works for you to feel as though no matter what this initial practice entails, you are not doing it wrong.

When I talk to people about starting meditation or giving it a try, I am shocked by the number of individuals that have tried something like this before. The number of people who have downloaded an app or saw a Facebook video that led them to give meditation a try. But most have not continued to stick with a daily program. Most individuals will tell me "oh well I really liked it, but I just stopped using the app" or "oh I wasn't good at meditation because I couldn't clear my mind." Even the people who have not even attempted it feel like they wouldn't "be good at it." It is answers like these that gave me the drive to try and talk to people about meditation, to try and dispel some of the rumors and show everyone that meditation is doable. If you are a living, breathing human being, you have the capacity to meditate.

Meditation is hot right now, it is like the avocado of the spiritual community. It is the thing that will cure everything, it will make you successful, and it might even give you super powers! These selling points have created a chain reaction leading to the emergence of phone apps, websites, retreat centers, and other money-making machines that try and market meditation as this incredible tool. While a lot of the benefits they proclaim are true, they don't get at the heart of meditation, at the reason for adding it into one's life. Rather it creates this film of obscurity, that has led to the answers I received from both people who have and have not attempted this practice. So instead of trying to add to the complexity by promising life changing results I simply want to showcase the individual beauty of this practice and let each person decide how it can impact his or her life.

Before I dive a little further into what this practice is, I want you to try and figure it out for yourself. I am going to provide some basic guidelines on posture and form and then I want you to experiment with a five-minute meditation. This is a quick session to help you start to see or continue to experience the beauty of meditation.

## HOW TO MEDITATE

Location

- You want to find a quiet place for your first meditation, one where you won't be distracted for this five-minute session.
- Though it is possible to meditate public places like a park or on the bus/subway, the distractions found here make the practice much harder.
- I would recommend that you try to limit all of your sensory inputs for this session, so it may help you turn off the lights and just use natural light. It is also helpful to limit other noises and distractions by shutting off: your phone, computer, TV, etc...

Posture

- Start by sitting in a position that is both relaxed and alert. You want it to be comfortable enough so you aren't struggling and in pain, but alert enough where you don't have to worry about falling asleep.

- he important boxes to check:
  - Have your spine straight
  - Your shoulders are relaxed
  - Your eyes can be closed or slightly open staring blankly in front of you
- Your hands can rest in your lap, or on your thighs
- This posture can be achieved in many forms, from the traditional lotus position with each foot on the opposite calf and the spine erect, to a desk chair meditation position, where you are sitting at your desk with your feet planted to the floor and your spine nice and straight.
- It is all about finding the position that is best to help you achieve this balance between relaxation and alertness.

## Breathing

- In this practice, we are going to try and focus on our breath.
- The premise, to try and notice you're breathing, trying to focus on what it feels like to breathe in and then breathe out.
- This is the goal of the entire practice, just to keep your attention on your breath, but as you will see this is much easier said than done.

## Distractions

- As thoughts and distractions start to arise, simply notice them, recognize that you are thinking.

- Once you realize that you are thinking, simply label the action as "thought" or "itch" or whatever it is.
- Then try and go back to the anchor, your breath. This is something you will do over and over again.

Now you're ready. So take five minutes and let's give it a try.

**

How was that for you?

Was it difficult? Was it easy?

What thoughts or feelings are you having right now?

I went through this same exercise with my 16-year-old sister one night. Right after we finished five minutes of meditation, I asked her how it went and she responded with "I didn't like all my thoughts," asking if I could make them go away. I tried to explain to her that thoughts are natural and asking the brain to stop thinking is like asking the heart to stop beating. While we cannot stop thoughts, we can watch them as if they are clouds floating through a clear blue sky; they are there but they are not the main point of focus on this beautiful sunny day. See your thoughts for what they are and try and return to the anchor of breathing.

This desire my sister expressed is often the case with a lot of people, they feel like they need to control their mind, ridding it of thoughts and emotions. But this idea is contrary to our human existence and contrary to the aim of meditation practice. Andy Puddicombe, co-founder of Headspace, one of the pioneering meditation phone apps, explains meditation as a way to step back and see your thoughts and emotions, to see what is going on in your life in this moment.

Andy explains, "Most people assume that meditation is all about stopping thoughts. Getting rid of emotions, somehow controlling the mind, but actually it's quite different from that. It's more about stepping back, sort of seeing the thought clearly, witness it coming and going, without judgement, but with a relaxed, focused mind."

Meditation allows us to see with greater clarity and without judgement, which in turn can lessen some of the stress and anxiety surrounding our thoughts. When we can step back and see our problems and our struggles, then we can do something about it; rather than living directly in them we can work through them.

There will be more on this later, but for now it is important to understand that **there is no such thing as a bad meditation**. Every time you sit down and step back, you are strengthening a muscle. It's just like working out. Even though some workouts will be better than others, each time you are in the gym is an opportunity to build a muscle and strengthen the body. The same is true for meditation, by sitting in full awareness, we strengthen our capability to see the world as it is in the present moment stripping away nagging thoughts that solely impede our ability to enjoy our existence.

# CHAPTER 3

# JUGGLING YOUR MIND

—

*"I think the present moment is underrated."*

— ANDY PUDDICOMBE, *FOUNDER OF HEADSPACE*

3:00 a.m. the alarm rings. Tenzin Gyatso rises from his bed in Dharmshala, India to begin his day. After a quick morning shower, he spends two hours in prayer, meditation and prostrations. At 5:00 a.m., he is out walking the residential premises, getting in a little exercise before breakfast.

His breakfast is light, usually some hot porridge and tea. During his meal, he will often turn on BBC in order to get his fill of the world news. He listens in English, and although it is not his native tongue, it is the language used by the majority of this planet, an audience he wishes to reach.

At 6:00 a.m., he returns to his morning meditation and prayers, devoting another three hours to the practice. By 9:00 a.m. most people in the world are at work, class or still asleep, but Tenzin has been awake for over 6 hours now. At this time he is often found studying various texts and commentaries trying to enhance his practice. At 11:30 am, he is found eating his last meal of the day, lunch. Following the strict rules of the monastery, he chooses not to eat dinner.

At 12:30 p.m., he goes into the office and is there for around three hours, doing interviews or talking to several audiences. At 5:00 p.m., he has his evening tea in preparation for another two hours of meditation and prayer. At around 7:00 p.m., His Holiness the 14th Dalai Lama otherwise known as Tenzin Gyatso retires for the night; he has another early morning the next day.

**

We are busy, we are all busy... even monks who are said to live very simple lives are busy. The world is a busy place and it can be extremely difficult to "live in the shit" as I like to say. Often it can be easier to reminisce about the past and think about good things to come in the future. But it can be very hard to stay in the present moment.

"When did you last take any time to do nothing? No emailing, no texting, no internet, no TV, no chatting, no eating, no reading, not even reminiscing about the past or planning for the future. Simply doing nothing." Andy Puddicombe begins his TED Talk in London with this question, reminding us that we often are so incredibly busy, we do not have the time to do nothing. Even when we complain about how busy we are, we still choose to do something in the little time we have. Frankly, aside from the time I do spend meditating it is hard to picture another time when I am doing absolutely nothing. Even if I am sitting in bed, I am often reminiscing or planning or lost in thought... or more likely watching Netflix.

So how in this environment where we spend our whole lives juggling, juggling our jobs and obligations, our family, our friends, our extra curriculars, going to the gym, social media, having a social life, eating, sleeping — how can we possibly find the time to do nothing?

The answer: Meditation.

Andy has this incredible analogy where he uses three juggling balls to explain meditation.

Throwing the balls in the air and catching them, he is able to, with ease, juggle while continuing to talk. He describes that in order to do so, he needs to find the right balance of relaxation and alertness, similar to the optimal posture for meditation. He explains that if he was too relaxed he would simply drop the balls unable to focus on the task at hand. But on the other side of the equation, if he was so focused on the juggling, he would start to get tense and be unable to continue speaking to the audience. So by finding the right balance between the two he is able to be in the present moment, juggling during his talk.

Often when we relax too much in a meditation, we find ourselves drifting off, lost in thought; we might even start to dose off, startled when the timer wakes us from our accidental slumber. And when we are too alert, trying too hard to meditate, we often struggle as well, unable to be in the moment, unable to sit with whatever is present, trying to force meditation rather than allowing it to occur naturally.

See if you can apply this analogy of juggling to your life… have you ever had a time where you felt like you were juggling too many things at once; where you felt as if you might just breakdown unable to keep going on.

For me, I recently started my first job out of college where I am working close to ten hours a day. I moved to a completely new city where I do not know a single person, and I am trying to finish writing a book. On top of that I try to go to the gym a handful of days per week and in order to save some extra money I try to cook most of my meals.

Right now for me it feels like I am juggling so many things. Sometimes it feels like I am going to drop them, like I am going to get so stressed out that I simply break under the pressure and can no longer do it. Or I am going to get too roped up in watching Netflix and surfing the internet, become too relaxed and forget my obligations.

At moments in these past few months, I have felt like a seesaw teetering between these two extremes. But for the majority of the time, I have managed to remain in the middle. I have managed to find the balance between relaxed and alert, to position myself in order to continue juggling all of my objectives.

How you may ask?

The answer again: Meditation.

Meditation has been an anchor for me that keeps me in the present moment. By taking time every day to do nothing, I feel like I can handle the overwhelming nature of life. I can handle the long hours of work and the new, unfamiliar environment. And whenever I feel like I can't I sit back down and focus on my breath trying to once again find that middle ground.

**⁑**

Andy Puddicombe explains how when we meditate, we start to realize our brains habitual patterns, we start to realize all of our thoughts, how many we have and how they are always present. A Harvard study confirms that we are lost in thought 47% of the time.[4] They further assert that this state of mind is highly correlated with unhappiness. This implies that we spend half our lives lost in thought, half our lives unhappy. Now a high school education will remind you that correlation doesn't equal causation, but this is still a shocking study that begs the question, what can we do about this? How can we prevent ourselves from being lost in thought?

Well, this starts with the initial recognition, the understanding that we are constantly thinking, that our brain is always running.

Andy shows how we have so many ways of thinking. Sometimes we are living just fine but there is that one thought that circles around and around. We often tend to reinforce that thought, encouraging it to continue.

For example if you have ever been unable to sleep and you sit there constantly repeating to yourself "I only have six hours

---

4    Bradt, S. 2010. "Wandering Mind Not A Happy Mind." *Harvard Gazette.*

to sleep, now five, now four." The hours start to count down as you keep reminding yourself you are unable to fall asleep. It is the continuous thought of sleep that prevents the oncoming slumber. If you simply just sat there in bed not trying to sleep, just accepting whatever your body was offering at the time, you would fall asleep more quickly.

Other times our brain can be mechanical, living a life that goes around and around, reminding ourselves to stay on our hamster wheel, a wheel that we thoroughly dislike. Waking up, eating, working, eating, working, eating, and sleeping. Instead of recognizing our dislike for this routine and finding the little moments to step off the wheel, we tend to think this is our fate, running on the wheel over and over until we have no energy left to keep moving.

Or sometimes we have that one nagging thought, the one that just pops up occasionally reminding us that we have yet to give this mindset attention, like an itch that you cannot seem to scratch.

With all these methods of thinking, the general takeaway is that our brain is always moving, we find that the mind is restless all of the time. Meditation provides the opportunity to see this, to recognize the mind's capacity and start to step back, to become comfortable with the thinking, understanding that we cannot change what happens but we can change the way we think about it. Sometimes we cannot stop juggling, we have to continue to maintain our life's obligations, but at least we can learn to find the middle ground. We can find a place between relaxation and alertness, a place where we can handle the pressures of life.

# CHAPTER 4

# THE SCIENCE OF MEDITATION

<hr/>

His Holiness the Dalai Lama supports the incredible impact of science as its understanding of meditation and its neurological impact develops. In his book, *The Universe in a Single Atom: The Convergence of Science and Spirituality,* The Dalai Lama goes even further to say that "if scientific analysis were conclusively to demonstrate certain claims in Buddhism to be false, then we must accept the findings of science and abandon those claims." This is a hefty proclamation, showing his willingness to put faith in science, to believe that science will only confirm what His Holiness believes to be the true: mediation has a profound impact on the human body and mind.

Even with the science, the most convincing evidence one will receive is from direct practice, the experience of sitting and meditating. While scientific evidence might help one start meditating, the direct experience will cause one to continue with the practice.

I and anyone else who has sat in practice can personally attest to the usefulness and impact of meditation, but it is extremely interesting to see the science support this fact.

## SCIENTIFIC ARGUMENT:

Meditation can:

- Increase happiness
- Increase memory
- Increase concentration
- Decrease stress
- Increase your immune response
- And much more…

It is widely agreed upon that the brain is moldable, or this notion of neuroplasticity. Simply put it is the idea that the neural networks of the brain can be continuously reshaped and by constantly repeating an action we can change the makeup of our brain. This can be seen in an MRI, where scientists can actually observe the neurons within the brain changing.

Dr. Sara Lazar wanted to know the physical impact of meditation on the brain. In her lab, Dr. Lazar performed an experiment on meditators, putting them in an MRI to see if there was a noticeable change in their brain structure. She was able to see that in meditators, both experienced and fairly new, there was an increased activity in two parts of the brain, gray matter locations one of which is correlated with happiness and the other memory.[5] This provides evidence for our point from Chapter One that meditation can make you a happier person not just when we talk about it logically, but also now there exists scientific evidence supporting the assertion that meditation can impact your happiness.

Other experiments have confirmed the same and more. It is widely understood that the left hippocampus, which is associated with memory and emotion regulation, is often less active in people who are depressed. But when those same people start meditating they see an increase in brain activity in this region.[6] In another study conducted at Johns Hopkins University, they were able to assert that meditation is as successful as antidepressants in reducing pain, anxiety, and depression.[7] This is an incredible revelation, which points

---

5   *Lazar, S. How Meditation Can Reshape Our Brains.* Filmed January 2012 in Cambridge, London. TEDxCambridge, 8:33.

6   Ibid.

7   Goyal, MD, Madhav, Sonal Singh, MD, and Eric Sibinga, MD. 2014. "Meditation Programs For Psychological Stress And Well-Being." *JAMA Internal Medicine.*

to the extremely positive impact of meditation, a tool that can cost no money and be accessed by anyone who has the ability to breathe.

**

Stress is one of the leading causes of death in our society. Whenever they interview anyone above the age of 100, asking them what their secret is, the common response always involves living a stress-free or low-stress life. They have found this to be the answer for both people who live extremely healthy lifestyles and others who smoke a handful of cigarettes and drink a glass of red wine every day.

I do not think that everyone should start drinking and smoking daily, but I do think that everyone should find the best way to reduce the stressors in their lives.

When we get stressed, we start to erode the telomeres or strands of DNA that are attached to the ends of our chromosomes. It is believed that the telomeres are responsible for the dividing and regeneration of cells and that erosion of them can lead to greater likelihood of cancer and death earlier in life.[8] According to Nobel Laureate, Elizabeth Blackburn,

---

8  Blackburn Ph.D., Elizabeth, Elissa Epel Ph.D., Jennifer Daubenmier Ph.D., Judith T. Moskowitz Ph.D. and Susan Folkman Ph.D. "Can

mindfulness and meditation can help prevent rapid degeneration of the telomeres. More on this will come later.

Dr. Lazar's lab provides further evidence that meditation decreases stress. Observing the amygdala, or the body's fight or flight response, Dr. Lazar was able to locate specific parts within this apparatus that are linked to states of increased stress. Creating the conditions for an experiment, her lab taught people meditation and then asked them questions regarding their stress levels.

These participants report much lower levels of stress than the control group, and MRI scans showed decreased activity in the stress correlated portion of the amygdala.[9] The participants did not have any change in their environment, they were still working and functioning in the same way as before, the only difference was the addition of twenty minutes of daily meditation, a tool that single-handedly decreased the stress levels of these individuals.

Everyone has heard the phrase "stress kills." We all know how bad stress is, but it is sometimes unavoidable, it is a part of life. Luckily, science is starting to point to meditation as a useful tool. A solution, to a once thought unsolvable problem.

---

meditation slow rate of cellular aging? Cognitive stress, mindfulness, and telomeres." *US National Library of Medicine.*

9  *Lazar, S. How Meditation Can Reshape Our Brains.*

But if you don't believe me, then to go back to the Dalai Lama's main argument, come and see for yourself. Take a seat, give it a try... you will see.

## LOOKING INSIDE THE BRAIN

Our minds form habits without recognition. It is part of our human capacity for our brain to recognize something as good or bad and then form a habit around obtaining or preventing that object.

If you don't believe me try crossing your arms.

No not like a mummy, as if you were angry.

Now try crossing them the other way.

It feels uncomfortable doesn't it! That is your body forming a habit around something as simple as crossing your arms.

Dave Mochel uses this exercise in his TED Talk to explain that our body will form habits without us even knowing. We simply get so accustomed to our individual way of doing things that any change feels extremely uncomfortable. One evening Dave was at the movies with his wife Marni. Enjoying the popcorn and the previews, Dave was excited to be in a stress free environment. At some point during the film, Dave felt an elbow in his side.

"Stop making that noise" Marni said in an annoyed whisper.

"What noise?" Dave responded.

"That weird noise you make when you breathe."

Dave had no idea what his wife was talking about. Turns out he had so much built up stress that his body formed the habit of loud breathing to try and release some of the stress. This is more common than one would expect.

I have a close friend who is stressed 24/7. He even stresses on vacation. He goes to a beautiful beach in the middle of the Caribbean and requires three days to simply settle in to the new relaxing lifestyle or "vacation mode" as he calls it. A day later, he is already thinking about going back to work and the stress comes back. Even when we try to avoid our habits by taking a vacation or unwinding with a glass of wine or a beer, our habits generally win.

What is actually happening here?

Dr. Judson Brewer, Director of Research and Innovation at the Mindfulness Center at Brown University and research affiliate at MIT, breaks it down showing that our mind creates habit loops that reinforce our behavior. For instance, when we eat something good like a piece of chocolate cake our brain says wow that was really good and because the food tastes good our brain tells us we feel good. Our brain then tries to remember the food, and exactly where we got it from, that way when we want to feel good, our brain can search through its rolodex and land on the tasty chocolate cake.

This mode of thinking is an evolutionary development that helped our ancestors survive when food was scarce; Dr. Brewer calls this "cave brain." Our ancestors would eat a piece of meat or berries and the brain would say "calories, survival!" This allowed our ancestors to remember where this food came from and what it looked like so they could survive.

However, today, we do not need to hunt for survival, so this mode of thinking is simply causing us to form habits, such as eating too much food. But it doesn't stop here, our brain is even smarter than just forming positive feedback loop—this is what Dr. Brewer uses to refer to the process above.

When something bad happens, our brain can go even further and solve the problem by getting something good. So if you fail a test, or get dumped, your brain will light up with the genius idea to make you crave chocolate cake as a way to help counteract the bad. Though this may sound good on the surface, it is actually a way of distracting ourselves from the actual problem at hand. Instead of dealing with the problems, we use things like binge eating, alcohol, and other mechanisms to help cope.

Trigger, behavior, reward.

This is the system that is hijacking our brain and forcing these habits to occur.

In our first example, we see chocolate cake (trigger) we think "oooh that looks good," we then eat the cake (behavior), and because it tastes good we feel good (reward).

This isn't a problem if it happens every now and then as everyone deserves to indulge a little. But if these habits start to overtake the conscious mind that is when the problem occurs. When you say you are going on a diet and you find yourself mindlessly eating chocolate cake the very next day, this is the habit taking over.

These habits aren't only formed around food. We form habits around stress management, sleeping, and as we saw even folding your arms is a habit. Some habits are good for us like brushing your teeth, others are just natural like folding your arms, and some are detrimental to physical and mental well-being like binge eating and smoking, the latter category is also referred to as addiction.

This is where meditation comes in. Meditation and further being mindful can help us "drive a wedge of awareness into our habit loops" as Dr. Brewer explains. This method allows us to step back and see clearly what we are getting from our behaviors, how they are helping or harming us. This understanding allows us to become disenchanted with our habits and ultimately let them go.

Dr. Brewer used this idea to create a program to help people overcome their bad habits. One of his most groundbreaking discoveries is that meditation and mindfulness can help people quit smoking. Dr. Brewer's method is almost five times as effective as therapy in getting smokers to quit.

His program is very different than most. Rather than ask smokers to put down the cigarettes immediately, he tells them to smoke. He looks smokers in the eye, smokers who came to him in order to quit and he tells them to smoke. The only corollary is just to pay attention, to be present with the smells, the feelings, and the sensations that come from smoking.

What do his participants realize?

That they don't really like smoking. That it smells bad, it tastes gross, and it is awful for them. One participant noticed that "even the sensation of putting the cigarette to her lips calmed [her] down," proving that smoking was actually a coping mechanism helping to reduce anxiety rather than an enjoyable hobby.

Her trigger was anxiety, her behavior was to smoke a cigarette, and her reward was she felt calm.

This is a habit loop running at full speed. But this same woman was able to quit.

She was able to become disenchanted with her habits by simply understanding how her brain was functioning. She, just like many other smokers, know the negative effects of smoking, but this doesn't help them quit. She had to go from knowing it in her head, or cognitively knowing that smoking is bad, to knowing it in her bones, feeling internally that smoking was not good for her.

Dr. Brewer works with individuals trying to help them overcome addictions. This is no easy feat, but he is finding his implementation of mindfulness, of having individuals pay attention to what is going on in the present moment without judgment, to be more effective than current outlets. But just like anything we do, there will be ups and downs and there is no guarantee that this will solve anyone's problem. Therefore, it is crucial to remember that every moment is an opportunity to get back on the wagon, to once again make a change for your own betterment.

Dr. Brewer told me a story about a man who joined the program hoping to change his relationship with drinking. This man would have 6–8 drinks a night just to help him fall asleep. Undergoing Dr. Brewer's mindfulness program, this man realized that the drinking was triggered by anxiety and the alcohol was a crutch, supporting him through the difficulties of his life. With this recognition, this man was able to slowly cut back and ultimately stop consumption all together. The man realized he didn't need booze to medicate himself, and rather he could open up to the world around him and experience it in the way that he wanted, not the way his habits had forced him to. This entire transformation only took a handful of weeks; fewer than 50 days and this man had overcome a lifelong addiction.

However, rarely do real life stories have a Hollywood ending and our protagonist did not ride off into the sunset with all of his problems being solved. Rather, he fell off this high and started to regress, going immediately back to the drinking as a crutch.

This regression mimics the New Year's diet phenomenon in our country. The most common New Year's resolution is to start a new diet or start exercising, yet people cannot seem to stick with the diet or the exercise for more than a few weeks. We so badly want to make a change but we cannot seem to do it. Everything goes fine until stress starts to take over our lives, until the feelings and emotions of life overcome the newness and freshness of the change.

What is happening here?

Stress shuts down the prefrontal cortex, the part of our brain that makes rational and conscious choices, defaulting to a more innate and habitual way of thinking. This is why when we get stressed we find ourselves returning to our habits, eating when we are not hungry, finishing a tub of ice cream only a week into our new diet or reaching for drink (or several) after a long day. Stress is the reason why our protagonist fell off the wagon and started drinking again.

My favorite phrases whenever I over-eat or return to a bad habit are: "tomorrow is a new day," or "fuck it I'll just go all out today and start again on Monday." It is a weird form of thinking, but often I push any big changes to the beginning of the week as if Monday's weren't already tough enough. But this does not have to be the case.

Dr. Brewer was not upset when he found out this man, who had come so far, had picked back up an old habit. Rather Dr. Brewer looked at him and said, "right now is the perfect time." The time to get back on the horse, to try again and again until we are able to gain control over our lives, until we are finally able to act in the way that we want in both times of ease and stress.

Dr. Brewer did not promise that his program would make one's problems, one's demons go away; rather his objective is to show people how the brain works so each individual can start to understand the inner workings of the mind. When we can both see and feel how our bodies are reacting, then we can actually make a change. But, this is not an overnight transformation; it is a lifelong journey of dealing with internal emotions, a journey that ends in individual growth, and a journey that will always be worth it.

# CHAPTER 5

# MOTIVATION TOWARD FAILURE

———

## SETTING A MOTIVATION

I like to start every meditation by setting a motivation, a reason for taking time out of my busy day to simply sit. Meditation is simple, but in no way is it easy; it is often an uphill battle to convince ourselves to sit down. We go back and forth in our heads constantly telling ourselves that there is a better use of our time, whether it be doing other work or even spending time on Facebook. We tend to be very good about talking ourselves out of things that we know will help us in the long run in favor of more immediate pleasures.

Lodro Rinzler, author of *The Buddha Walks into a Bar*, describes us as an instant gratification society, desiring to immediately get what we were promised. I mean it is very true, we will often get mad when our Amazon package is not there within two days. Ultimately, with meditation, there is a much longer timeline to gratification. It is as if you went to the gym once and expected to already lose 10 lbs. It is just not going to happen like that. You aren't going to just meditate once and immediately achieve total serenity and bliss for the rest of your life. It is going to take effort, and constant repetition, of sitting down every day and practicing.

Like many things in our lives, this practice is easy to give up. It is so easy to just go through the motions of the day and before you know it, it is midnight and you are in bed having forgotten to meditate. Then this starts to become our pattern, we always say we want to integrate something new into our daily routine, but it is hard to make the time. It is much easier to default to doing just what we have to do and not everything we want to do.

One of my favorite examples is when I tell myself I am going to start studying for an exam a week in advance and make a study guide so I won't have to do everything the night before. Gosh, it would be so nice to be prepared; it would make my life so much easier. But often without fail,

I find myself opening my notebook the night before the test looking at the material for the first time and being forced to cram it all into my brain, increasing my stress levels and decreasing the amount of sleep I can get.

How can we fix this?

How can we motivate ourselves to do things that will help us but aren't really necessary in our daily routine; how can we motivate ourselves to meditate?

Well, the answer is in the question, we need to set a motivation, a reason for why we are doing this.

**Every time I sit down to start a meditation, I set a motivation, I think about why I am sitting. What is the reason for waking up early and making the time to practice?**

It does not have to be the same motivation every time, but it needs to be strong enough to keep you with the practice of meditation. Whatever your motivation is, whether you want to be a better person, or learn to be more relaxed, think of that every time you sit down and it will remind you why you are here why you are making this part of your life.

I have often heard objections to this idea, saying that a goal will simply get in the way of meditation. For example, if you say you are going to sit in order to become calmer, then you will be fixated on the desire to become calm that you will walk away from your meditation feeling anything but calm. This is a valid objection that reminds me of the sleep example of being unable to sleep and the continuous fixation on trying to sleep makes you stay up even later.

So in line with this, the motivation for our meditation is only supposed to help us settle into the cushion, to keep us practicing, but once we are sitting, we can let go of everything including this motivation and give way to the practice. Allow yourself to use the motivation, but do not let the motivation control you.

It is very important to set a motivation. If you have ever tried to get in shape you would know that without a goal in mind it is hard to convince yourself to get to the gym on those difficult days. Your goal might be the desire to shed a few pounds and get some greater definition for your abs, or because it feels good and makes you happy. This motivation will drive you to the gym, but often once the workout starts, you get lost in the adrenaline or the routine of the exercise and are not fixated on the motivation itself.

For meditation, this is the same goal, to let the motivation drive us but not consume us.

So take a minute right now and think, why are you here, why do you want to learn how to meditate, or continue to deepen an already established practice? Think about it and think about how it makes you feel, if it is really a good motivator, it will make you want to sit, it will give you that drive, that extra push on the hard days.

## THE GOAL

So what is my motivation? Well as I explained in the beginning, this book is about much more than just meditation. This is a call for happiness, a desire for change at the individual level, leading to a domino effect that can change the entire world.

I had a therapist who always said, "Hurt people, hurt people."

But what if 7 billion people were all happy within their own skin?

Would there still be war or conflict? Would we still want to hurt others?

Or would we feel the need to simply embrace our fellow humans realizing that we are all very similar on the inside?

In Howard Cutler's book *The Art of Happiness*, co-written with the Dalai Lama himself, His Holiness makes the assertion that as human beings we are far more similar than different. Every human being has an innate desire to be happy and to avoid suffering. Even though on the surface, we can see so much division, so much divide between people based on race, ethnicity, social status, sexuality, religion and so much more, we can all be connected by our desire to find happiness. This is a desire that goes far deeper than all of our divides, and the recognition of this can be a reason for us to feel united.

So why write this book? What is my goal, my motivation? I want to change the world; I want to show that all humans are more connected than separate and show the need for us all to help one another, to live with our similarities and not our differences.

**

Most of the time when I start my sit, my motivation sounds something like this:

"I am sitting to make myself a better person, a better person for myself and for others, building my traits of compassion, patience, and love so that I can spread this to those around me."

By bettering myself, I can be a better person to those in my life and those in the world. It is this idea that gets me to the cushion each morning and helps me to settle in, reminding me why I am doing this.

I hope to spread this sentiment to you reading this book. Not just teaching you about a meditation regimen, but also showing you a method of gaining control over your own happiness of realizing that you are in control of yourself and with this you too can change the world.

By simply being happier, you will spread happiness. By being more patient, you will spread patience. So, we develop this practice not just for ourselves but for all of those we love, all of those we do not know, and even those we struggle with.

**Changing the world starts within each and every one of us and I believe that we can have an impact.**

The Buddha once said, "Thousands of candles can be lighted from a single candle, and the life of the candle will not be shortened. Happiness never decreases by being shared."

So keep reading, keep learning and see that with these tools we can start to better understand our own minds, which in turn will allow us to understand the minds of others, creating a greater understanding and compassion towards every person in this world. This isn't going to happen overnight, but I truly believe that we will change the world. It may be my goal, but I cannot do it without you.

## THE F WORD

Failure, the mother fucking "F Word." Yeah that's right I said it... FAILURE. This is something that all of us as humans struggle with. It is in our DNA to fail. I mean if you really think about it, our bodies will eventually fail and be unable to sustain our life any longer. This fate sets the stage for a state of mind that we are all too familiar with: failure.

Failure can be debilitating. Anyone who has ever failed a test of a quiz knows that receiving that verdict is not one that you can easily bounce back from. You don't look at the grade and immediately think, wow I need to do better next time, let's start finding ways to achieve this new goal. No, rather we tend to beat ourselves up, blaming ourselves, blaming the test or the class, doing anything to avoid the actual problem at hand. Failure can be so debilitating that the fear of failure can prevent you from even attempting something you desire, let alone succeed at it.

However, I believe that failure itself is not scary.

**Failure, simply put is iterations at success.**

It is the attempts that lead up to an ultimate victory. Failure is just a practice run. In order to achieve success, failure is a necessity. So therefore, the only thing getting in the way is not failure itself, but the fear of failing. This is what I am concerned with: the feelings that impede effort, a fear that prevents us from doing the things that are important to us or the things that we want to do.

I have heard too many times people tell me that they have tried meditation and they just weren't good at it, that they couldn't do it, or that they tried and failed. Well that is all part of the process, without failure we wouldn't know what success would look like. But, funnily enough, unlike most things in life, meditation is very hard to fail at, for every single time you sit down to give it a try is a success.

It is very easy to be scared to fail. It is very easy to convince yourself that you wouldn't be good at meditation, or it wouldn't be right for you or any other excuse that could prevent you from attempting something that might truly help you. So I am not going to tell you how to succeed at meditation, I am going to show you that it is okay to fail in life, and that failure is necessary and imperative to our ultimate success.

*"I've missed more than 9000 shots in my career. I've lost almost 300 games. Twenty-six times, I've been trusted to take the game*

*winning shot and missed. I've failed over and over and over again in my life. And that is why I succeed."*

– MICHAEL JORDAN

Almost every single time we fail, there is a lesson learned. It might not come right away or be the easiest to understand but lying under all of that self-doubt and defamation is a lesson, a teaching from which you can learn. So instead of feeling sorry for yourself and making yourself out to be the victim, accept your failure, accept that it is just part of the journey.

The biggest problem that I see in helping people build a meditation practice is the inability to continue meditating. Often times people are more than willing to give it a try, but one bad session or one difficult state of mind can push you as far away from the practice as you can possibly imagine. Often it can feel as if a practice that was so helpful at one point is just no longer working. It can feel like meditation just isn't for you or that you are simply not any good at it.

I have been in this exact position myself. When I starting meditating, I thought it was the best thing I had discovered in a long time, that it was one of the most useful, insightful, and life changing practices that I had ever come across. Yet for some reason, I could not convince myself to do it. I remember, day after day I would get into bed with the realization that I had not meditated that day. I would tell myself that the next day would be different and try to get up early or stay up later and fit it in, but time after time, I would get back into bed the next day with the same feeling of failure.

So what did I do? How did I convince myself that I needed to make this part of my daily routine? How did I make the time for this practice with all of the other things on which I was focused? Well my trick was I made it my own. I made the practice mine. I learned as much as I could and then I set the parameters for myself. I decided how long I wanted to meditate for, what type of meditation I wanted to do, why I wanted to do it, where I wanted to do it. I put so much of myself into the practice that I simply couldn't fail.

You know when people ask you to explain yourself in several sentences. Well I was dealing with this question frequently, as I would constantly meet new people in college. Meditation became one of the words that I used the most in describing who I am. Even though I wasn't yet practicing every day, I wanted it to be something that defined me, for I felt happiest when I was engaging in the practice. It got to a point where if I wasn't meditating I felt like I wasn't myself. It became such an integral part of my character that it became me.

I went from a guy who meditates to the meditation guy.

See if I failed at this practice, then I was failing at being myself. I had made this practice a part of me and there was no way I was going to fail at being me. And even when I did, even when I would miss a day, I wouldn't get down on myself I would just remember that tomorrow was a new opportunity. An opportunity to succeed once again.

That being said, it was not a seamless transition. It wasn't like all of a sudden I was just a meditation guru, frankly I am nowhere near that, but I stopped being afraid to fail. I started to be okay with trying the practice and not being upset if I didn't enjoy it one day or if it was difficult for me. I realized that I can keep on trying; I can keep finding what works for me and my practice.

Meditation is not one size fits all, at the end of the day it is your life, your journey, and you need to make it yours. You need to figure out what it is going to take to make it so that you can fail, to fail with grace so that one day you can ultimately succeed. You need to make this practice you.

## YOUR JOURNEY

Although we are all on this path together, this journey is one that no one can do for you. You are on a path of individual discovery and while you will receive help and guidance along the way, only you can do the work. This is why it is imperative to find what works for you. Start with your own motivation and end with a practice that you can sustain and that works for you.

In this book, I try to present a variety of information that I have learned along my journey. But as I've said, my journey is still going and I am still learning with each new moment. With this in mind, don't take me at my word. If I present a type of meditation claiming that "this is the best meditation you can do and if you want to make a million dollars you should start this meditation today," while this may sound pretty promising, it may not work for you. So try things out, read more on the things that interest you; if you get confused, seek teachers who will explain it in a way that you can understand, and experience all that the world of meditation has to offer.

This is your journey and you need to be the one to run it, but by no means are you alone. There are thousands of other people on this road with you all wanting you to succeed, wanting you to be truly happy and content. But they will not put you on their backs and carry you across the finish line. That you need to do for yourself.

So let's get started.

# PART II

## LEARNING
## A LOT

*"There is no way to happiness – happiness is the way."*

– THICH NHAT HANH

# CHAPTER 6

# STARTING FROM SCRATCH, BUILDING A PRACTICE

———

Matthieu Ricard is considered the happiest man in the entire world.[10]

Matthieu Ricard is a French born, Buddhist Monk, who holds a unique title as the world's happiest individual. He got this title after partaking in a science experiment that looked at the activation of different parts of the brain. They found that by looking at the activation of the right prefrontal cortex vs. the left prefrontal cortex, they could

---

10 "The Buddhist Monk And Author Matthieu Ricard May Be The World's "Happiest Man," According To Science". 2017. *Business Insider.*

hypothesize how happy an individual was. They found that the stronger the activation of the left side, the more an individual reported being happy, having positive states of mind, joy, higher energy, more enthusiasm, and more. When Matthieu participated in this study, he was reported as having the highest activation of the left-prefrontal cortex they had measured. This awarded him the title of the world's happiest man.

Mindfulness guru and Author of *Search Inside Yourself*, Chade-Meng Tan makes the joke "that we could imagine Matthieu was thinking of something particularly naughty." But really what is revealed is that during this experiment, Matthieu was meditating on compassion.

Compassion meditation or loving-kindness meditation, also called metta meditation, is one practice in which many meditators engage. Often people think meditation is one specific thing, one practice that often refers to sitting and doing nothing. People are often shocked to find out how many different techniques and practices fall under the meditation umbrella.

The best way to think about it is to consider meditation like training for a sport. Let's take soccer for example. If you said you were training for soccer, it could mean that you were doing strength training, cardiovascular training, and actual drilling of the sport, maybe even mental training. Meditation is very similar, there are many different ways to train the mind and loving-kindness meditation is one example. In this section, I am going to explain some different types and styles of meditation in hopes of helping you build your meditation toolkit, adding different strategies to build that mental muscle.

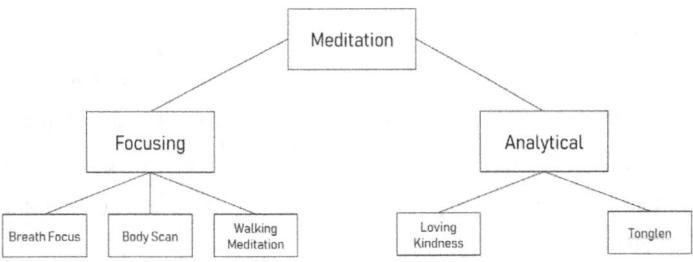

For the purposes of this book I have divided meditation into two big categories. And as you can see from the chart below, these categories breakdown into the more specific practices that we can do. These are just a few of many.

As I go through and explain all of these practices, try to do the ones that stand out to you. Don't feel any pressure to do them all. I just want you to see the extent of this practice and hopefully one will work for you.

## CONCENTRATION PRACTICES

The definition of a concentration practice is found within the title itself. These are often practices where we use one object as the focal point of our meditation, as our anchor.

Often the goal is to concentrate on this object and when thoughts arise to distract us, we are supposed to try to let go of these, returning to the object at hand.

The point is to create a more focused mind, something that we can all benefit from. A focused mind is a powerful mind. Just think about how much more you can accomplish without distractions, and imagine being able to do this at all times.

## BREATH FOCUS

We have already gone over breath focus meditation. This was the initial practice that I had you try in the beginning of this book.

Object of Concentration: The Breath

Distractions: Thoughts, sensations, sounds...

Goal: to try to focus on our breath, and when other thoughts arise, simply let them go and return to the breath.

## BODY SCAN

A body scan is a meditation technique in which we bring focus and attention to our bodies, scanning the different limbs and muscles, trying to find where we might hold tension or stress.

Object of concentration: The Body

Distractions: Sounds, thoughts…

Goal: To scan through the body, focusing our attention on the different parts to see if we can find any tension or stress. When we get distracted, just return the attention to the body.

Body scans are a wonderful technique that help us to connect more to what is going on within our body. The premise behind this idea is that every emotional and mental state can be connected to a physical sensation within the body. When we can sit with these physical sensations, we can learn more about the emotional and mental state.

Doing a body scan:

- This practice can be done sitting in a meditative posture or even laying down
- Start by settling in and trying to first bring your attention to your breath as if we were doing the breath focus meditation.

- Now once you have started to settle into the space, shift your attention from your breath to the toes on your left foot.
  - What sensations do you feel?
  - Is there tingling? Is there pain? Is there tension?
- Slowly make your way down your toes into your foot, up the foot and into the ankle, all the while keeping this sentiment of inquiry.
- Make your way up your left leg, feeling sensations in the calf, the thigh, the hip. Then shift your attention to the toes on your right foot, repeating the same process.
- Afterward, start to make your way up your arms, starting with the fingers of the left hand and ending with the shoulder on the right.
- Shifting your attention try and focus on the feelings in your torso, your abdomen, your chest. Often we can hold tension in these locations so look for that and just try to feel it.
- We then bring our attention up our neck and to our face, feeling all of the muscles in the face: our jaw, our mouth, lips, nose, cheeks, eyes, brows, forehead... all the way to the crown of our head.
- Finally try to feel your entire body all at once, feel any sensations that present themselves and just notice them, don't try to change anything.
- In this practice we are not trying to change or avoid any of the sensations that we feel, rather we just want to sit with them, accepting that this is what is happening, right here right now and that is okay.

## WALKING MEDITATION

Walking meditations are a great addition to any practice. When you first start meditating, often it can be physically taxing to sit for long periods. Walking meditations are a great way to enhance your practice while you are still working on building the muscles needed to sit for long periods.

Object of concentration: The act of walking

Distractions: Thoughts, sounds, images...

Goal: To try to tune into the present moment and our bodies by walking, focusing on the act of walking, taking one step at a time, with no other goal in mind.

How to do a walking meditation:

- Find a place where you have enough space to walk, I would say 50 square feet or so should give you more than enough room as walking back and forth is not against the rules. Try to find a place that is free of obstacles and perhaps one that is quiet and isolated, especially if this is your first time with this practice.
- The concept here is the same as the other concentration practices, we are going to bring our focus to a specific object and try to remain focused on that object. If we happen to lose focus, we will gently remind ourselves to return to the task at hand.

- So start by standing up nice and straight, taking some deep breaths in trying to settle into the space.
- Then start with an inhale. As you breathe in lift one foot into the air. Feel the sensations of pushing off the ground, the muscles moving in perfect harmony. Feel the entire process as you slowly start to lower the foot onto the ground in front of you, exhaling as you make contact with the ground.
- This process should feel fluid, so if you need to a take a few breaths per step or a few steps per breath, that is okay, just try and be present with the sensations and feelings of walking. As meditation teacher, Thich Nhat Hanh puts it, "Walk as if you are kissing the Earth with your feet."
- This should not be a stroll but rather try to bring a careful attention to the act of walking. So it will often require you to walk a lot slower than usual.

## ANALYTICAL MEDITATIONS

Analytical meditations have a different focus. The premise is that within all of us lie insights, wisdom, and understanding that are waiting to be revealed.

In analytical meditations, we use our mind to analyze topics and try to learn more about them. These are often deep topics like understanding commonalities among human beings, or trying to increase your capacity for patience and kindness. Analytical meditations are great and can really help us to understand more about our world and ourselves. They also require a personalized element, and as you will see in many of them, it is best to visualize friends and family in order to make the meditations more real for you.

There are many different forms of analytical meditations and they can be utilized in many different ways. For the sake of this book, I am only going to describe the few with which I am most familiar.

## LOVING KINDNESS MEDITATION

Matthieu Ricard does a wonderful job of explaining loving kindness meditation, and how much of an impact it can have.

Question of Comprehension: How to increase my capacity for love and kindness?

Goal: Learning how to increase this capacity for both myself and for others.

As you can see, analytical meditations are slightly different. Rather than trying to focus around a central point, letting thoughts pass, we are trying to use thought to better understand a concept.

How to practice loving kindness meditation like the happiest man in the world:

- We start the same way, by taking some deep breaths and cultivating a state of mind that is both relaxed and alert.
- You start by cultivating an image of someone you love unconditionally. This can be someone you know or maybe even imagining a small, innocent child.
- When you have that person in your mind, simply try and feel nothing but love for him or her, showering that individual in a warm embrace that surrounds and engulfs them.
- In Matthieu Ricard's explanation, this becomes the object of your meditation, the central point that you return to. If that feeling of love and embrace starts getting dull, try and make it more vivid. If it fades, bring it back into focus, trying to fill yourself with love and compassion.
- Often times this exercise can involve wishing well on the person you are visualizing saying in your head: "may you experience love," or "may you experience kindness."
- As our practice continues, we slowly start to move away from the people we love unconditionally and try to cultivate this feeling for all of our friends, then strangers and finally the people we struggle with the most. No one should be exempt from our kindness.
- By simply cultivating this sentiment of love and kindness for other individuals we end up creating greater happiness for

ourselves; for it is said, that we are happiest when we are doing things for other people.

So as you may be thinking, there is definitely some overlap between the analytical type and focusing type meditations, as there is still an object of focus in both practices. The only difference is that in the analytical meditation, we are using thoughts.

During the loving kindness practice, we use our mind to think about love. We wish for others and ourselves to experience feelings of kindness.

## TONGLEN

This practice is one of my very favorites. It is a practice called *Tonglen*, which in Tibetan translates to *giving and taking*. It is by no means an easy practice, but it is extremely powerful. This practice can be very emotional and needs to be approached with an open mind and a big heart.

Tonglen:

- We start the same way, by taking some deep breaths and cultivating a state of mind that is both relaxed an alert.
- Call to mind an individual in your life, maybe a person who you consider a good friend (it is often easier to start this

practice with a person who doesn't have the biggest emotional weight in your life).

- Picture that person sitting in front of you and try to think about the hardships, the suffering that this person goes through on a daily basis.
- Imagine that this suffering is filling their entire body and that they are in desperate need of help, help that only you can provide.
- As you continue to breathe, imagine that your inhales are slowly sucking the suffering out of the other person. Visualize that suffering in the form of black smoke, smoke that clouds the air above the other individual.
- Take a few breaths, clearing that individual completely of all of their suffering, picturing a big cloud of thick, black smoke in the air above you both.
- Pause and look into yourself. Picture a hard black rock right above your heart. This is an embodiment of the negativity and suffering that you yourself feel on a daily basis.
- Looking back at the smoke, take a deep breath, intending to take all of that smoke into yourself. Let that smoke collect at your heart where that rock is, dissolving the rock into the cloud of smoke.
- Exhaling, imagine both the smoke from the cloud above you and the smoke from the dissolved rock, leave your body.
  - The goal here is not to take on the suffering of the other individual, but to use this practice to expel the suffering from both you and that person.

- You are left sitting with a shining white light that fills your entire body. It is a light that fills you with joy and happiness. It is the embodiment of warmth and compassion that invades every inch of your person.
- As you breathe out, share this light, push this light to the person in your mind, until they too are completely filled and surrounded by the white light. Sit with this image for a few moments and then let this person fade.
- Repeat the practice but try it with someone who you find difficult, see if you can cultivate this same desire for an individual you struggle with.

The goal of this practice is to realize that compassion can be cultivated. That you can look at another individual and want to rid them of suffering and leave them with nothing but joy and warmth. It is within this practice that we can test out this idea and then in real life we try to actually implement it by meeting difficult situations and people with nothing but compassion.

**

There are many more variations of meditation, each with unique techniques and processes. But all of these are aiming towards the same goal: to help you be a happier and more content person in the present moment.

By developing our focus, we learn to be more present. By bringing compassion and love into our meditation practice we are able to view others in a different light and have a positive impact on both the world and ourselves. Meditation has the capacity to do this for you, for anyone.

For the time being, we will start slowly, building up a practice that you can eventually call your own. Feel free to experiment with the practices I have just explained but for now, let's go back to our very simple beginning practice of breath focus. This is where we will spend most of our focus during this book as it is the perfect place to start.

The breath is always present and soon we will be too.

## DIVING DEEPER INTO BREATH FOCUS

Focusing on the breath is a lot harder than it seems. If you have just tried meditation for the first time while reading this book, you will know this to be the case. If you are a seasoned professional at this point, you will remember the difficulty during your first sessions, a difficulty you might still be facing.

This can often be a surprise to many people.

If I told you that I would pay you $100 for every minute that you could spend focusing only on your breath, you would tell me challenge accepted thinking that you just entered the best money making scheme of your life.

However, after about a few seconds, you will most likely find yourself distracted, thinking about something else.

Bottom line, this practice is not easy. Focusing on your breath is hard, but here are some tips to make it easier.

How to Focus on the Breath:

- Most of the time when we think about focusing, the method goes something like this… you try really, really hard to keep your attention in one place, you may even notice your eyes tightly closed and the constant repetition in your head of "I need to focus on my breath, I need to focus on my breath…" This process is very self-defeating.
- Focusing should be effortless, almost as if you are gently resting your attention on your breath in a manner that you would use to place a baby into its crib.
- What do I mean by this? Basically, you have to find the difference between focusing on the breath cognitively and feeling the breath on a much deeper level.
- So take a deep breath in right now. Notice that you can feel the breath coming in. You can feel it in four places:
    - **The tip of your nose**: if you focus, you can feel the cooling sensation of the air as it enters through your nose.

- ○ **The back of your throat**: as the air makes its way into your body, you can feel a slight coolness and tingling sensation in the back of your throat.
- ○ **The chest**: as you breathe in, and your lungs fill with air, your chest expands and contracts.
- ○ **The stomach**: as the breath makes its way down the throat and into your stomach, you can feel the air inflate your stomach as if it were a balloon.
- By focusing on one of these locations, you can feel the breath enter and exit your body. Rather than trying desperately to keep the focus, you can gently place your attention on one of these locations.
- Try all four and find which works best for you.

This will not change your practice overnight, but it will point you in the right direction of making the process more effortless.

**

Once we can focus on our breathing, we can give attention to the second part of the practice — trying to let go of distractions, thoughts, and sensations that try to tear you away from the present moment.

Distractions are unavoidable, but it can often be very difficult when we notice them. We can often feel defeated and feel like we aren't good at meditation.

But that is the opposite of the truth.

Noticing distractions is a huge victory in meditation, for a second ago you were lost in thought and now you are recognizing this and returning to the present moment. Recognizing distractions is an incredible achievement for it allows us to return to the present moment.

Distractions will come, I promise you that they will come; even after meditating for years; distractions can still manifest their way into our minds. We have spent our entire lives thinking about a plethora of different things, so it will naturally be difficult to try to rid ourselves of this with just a few 5-minute meditation sessions. But there are tips and tricks to help deal with distractions, to feel as if you can let them go and return to the present moment.

How to deal with distractions:

- When you notice a distraction, the key is not to get upset, not to be disappointed in yourself and your meditation. Rather think of this as a success story, for now you can do something about it.

- Try to label the distraction. For example, if I catch myself thinking about what I have to do for the rest of the day, I would label that "planning" and then try and return to my breathing.
- The point of labeling is to prevent us from chasing our thoughts. In trying fully to identify my distraction, I might follow it down its chain, thinking about where it came from, why I am thinking about this thing until I am distracted by my distraction.
- The label is a quick way to recognize the distraction and then simply return to the anchor of your practice that in this case is the breath.

**

Finding the place between relaxed and alert:

Meditation is all about finding the middle ground. As stated in our initial explanation, your posture needs to be in a state between relaxation and alertness. Well, this sentiment should not be reserved for just our posture. As we saw in Chapter Three with the juggling analogy, we should further strive to also find this balance in our minds, find the place between relaxation and alertness.

When we are too relaxed, it can lead to sleep. If we are too alert, we tend to try too hard, stress, then force meditation rather than letting it happen.

Tara Brach in her short book, *How to Meditate,* provides some incredible insight on finding this middle ground.

Too alert?

During the course of a normal day, we, as human beings, do not use the full capacity of our lungs. We have grown accustomed to taking these short breaths in and out.

The effect of this is we feel like we are holding onto shit. Whether it be emotional baggage, or anxiety, when our breath is short, we cannot release enough of life's pressures.

Think about it. When do you normally experience shortness of breath?

Well aside from working out, this feeling comes when we are hyperventilating, crying, scared, or experiencing other strong emotions. It can be very uncomfortable to sit when this is the background noise of our life.

- When this is the case, put an increased emphasis on your exhalation. When you focus on breathing out, you inherently relax.
- So take a deep breath in, and let it out, trying to empty your full lung capacity, relaxing the shoulders, and feeling yourself naturally get lighter.

- Continue to do this practice when you find that you are unable to just let meditation occur naturally.
- The process should be effortless and this trick can help with that.

Too relaxed?

Often our bodies are not used to doing nothing. The only other data point our brain has for this state is sleep. That is the only activity that the brain has to associate with the feeling of shutting down the engine that is running at all times.

Therefore, it can be very natural to get tired and feel sleepy during your practice.

When this is the case, it is great to focus on the in-breath. Take big breaths in to try to get more oxygen to your brain and your muscles.

- There are many different breathing techniques that can help to stimulate the brain and awaken us.
- Focusing on the inhale is a great one, breathing in, try to fill your lungs to their capacity. Hold the breath in for a second and then let it all out.

Breathing is often something we take for granted, but when we give it our full attention, we realize the capacity it has, all of the things that we can do just with our breath.

**

What about when I have an itch?

Often when we sit still, we realize all of the itches and scratches that arise. It can feel like our body is itchier than normal as we are now less distracted.

Itches and other sensations can also be distractions; they can pull us away from the present moment and drive us crazy. They can also be a great instructor and a perfect example of how to let go of attachments.

- When an itch arises, first try not to scratch it and treat it as a distraction: label it "itch" and then return focus to the breath.
- If it persists, then sit with it. If you simply cannot get your attention off the itch, then make it the object of your meditation.
- This might sound crazy but when you do this, you will realize that like all things in this world, an itch has a beginning middle and end, as eventually it will go away. In this sense, these annoying distractions can actually teach you something pretty incredible.

- If you still are unsuccessful and it continues to drive you crazy, then scratch it. However, do it mindfully almost as if you were practicing itching meditation. Feel your hand move towards the sensitive location. When you are there try to pause, feeling the sensation for one last second and then scratch away, all the while paying attention to what that feels like.

I am sure you never thought someone could talk about an itch for so long. Nevertheless, everything that arises during your meditation is a lesson, is an opportunity to deepen your practice. So treat everything with care.

## SETTING A TIMER

In the beginning of my practice, I found that the timer was one of my biggest distractions. The second that the timer popped into my head, my meditation practice was over. Instead of focusing on my breath, the timer became the object of my focus. I would sit there and think, how much time do I have left and go through calculations in my head of how long it has been, until finally, the bell brought me back to reality and my time was up.

This made my meditation feel like it was never-ending. 5 minutes felt like 30 and 20 minutes felt like a lifetime. It made meditation a chore rather than an enjoyable practice.

One day I decided not to set a timer. I figured I would just sit and meditate for as long as I could. After what seemed like 10 minutes, I got up feeling great, feeling like I had meditated for just the right amount of time. Much to my surprise, 25 minutes had gone by!

This reminded me of a chapter I had read in one of my favorite childhood books *Touching Spirit Bear.* It is a novel about a young boy who is sent to an island as part of his juvenile rehabilitation program. Part of his daily routine required him to soak in a cold pond every morning. On his first soak, his teacher tells him, sit for as long as you need no more and no less. By this the teacher meant, do not fixate on how much time you need to dedicate to things, rather do them until their completion, until you feel ready to stop.

It was unbelievably rewarding to do this with my meditation. I had such a feeling of freedom as if I wasn't constrained by anything and I could just be.

However, in our crazy busy world where we live, it is hard to just say I will sit for as long as I need. Often the fear is that you may sit for too long and miss certain commitments. So it is hard not to set a timer.

"But how much time should I start out with?" I get this question often, from people who are first starting to meditate.

How long should they meditate? Well, the answer isn't a clean hard number like most people desire. No two people are identical and while some may struggle with meditation and feel it to be a taxing and draining process, others might find this practice to be more natural.

I think that the best strategy for finding a time that you can commit to is by sitting and starting a stopwatch. See how long you can comfortably sit in meditation and have that be your benchmark. Even if it is only thirty seconds to start out, that is totally fine.

Every person will get something different out of meditation and you need to keep finding what works best for you.

## MINDFULNESS

The popularity of this word has increased greatly over the last few years. Mindfulness, it is almost like a brand, like organic, or back to our previous example, the avocado, of the mental health space. With so much out there surrounding this word, it is easy to find the wrong applications and people looking to use it for their own personal advancement, using it just to make money. However, mindfulness does not need to be sold, or difficult to explain, really its purpose is quite simple. But, as you may have caught onto by now, simple does not mean easy.

Mindfulness as explained by Jon Kabat-Zinn, the creator of Mindfulness-Based Stress Reduction, is simply "paying attention to the present moment, on purpose, without judgment." This is really a beautiful definition because it implies that anything can become the object of our meditation. Whether we are sitting, walking, or eating, we can pay attention to that moment, enhancing our practice.

I like to think about mindfulness as meditation applied off the cushion—a term meditators use to refer to life spent outside of formal seated meditation. By paying attention to each moment we can implement meditation into everything we do.

Why do we need to be mindful; why should we pay attention to the present moment? Well, let's think of an example.

If you have ever driven a car, you will know that it is very hard to pay attention in the present moment. Yes, this sounds horrible as every one of us had to pass a test that showed our ability to pay attention while we are behind the wheel, but the longer we spend driving the more confident we are in our ability to drive mindlessly.

Think back to what it was like to drive for the first time. Think about how nervous you were, how cautious you were. More than likely you had two hands on the wheel. You had your eyes on the road in front of you with the radio off. You were focused purely on the action of driving.

Fast forward a few years. Now you have one hand on the wheel, the radio blasting, and you are probably zoned out thinking about a plethora of other things, not focused on the task at hand.

I am guilty of this too. I have gotten confident in my driving abilities and feel like I no longer need to truly give my full attention to driving.

I am sure we all have experienced the following: you are driving somewhere and you happen to have a lot on your mind. You are still paying attention to the road, but before you know it, you are passing your exit on the highway or missing the turn that you need to make.

You might have to reconfigure your route, which is mostly just an inconvenience. But you might try and react and swerve off the highway into the exit lane, or try and right turn at an unsafe speed. This reaction, which I am sure many of us have attempted, is extremely dangerous, putting both our own lives and the lives of others in danger.

What if instead, we paid a little closer attention to the task at hand? If instead of zoning out during the drive, we gave it our full attention? We would not only get where we want to faster, but we would also be a responsible and safe driver for the world and ourselves.

**

This is just a small example, but it demonstrates a much larger point. Meditation should not be reserved just for the time spent on the cushion; rather our entire life should be spent in the present moment.

Often when starting to meditate, we practice for anywhere from 5 minutes to an hour every day, but what are we supposed to do for the other 23 hours. If we are really trying to become more comfortable with our own minds and learn things about ourselves, it would seem counter-intuitive to just do five minutes and then live the rest of the day back on autopilot. It would be like starting to workout but still eating poorly and living an unhealthy lifestyle. So just like starting to live a physically healthy lifestyle, we need to live a mentally healthy lifestyle and be mindful at all times not just during meditation.

## MINDLESSNESS

Isn't it hard to be mindful all the time?

My mom asked me this question one day, wondering if it was okay to be "mindless" every now and then.

For me, the answer is no.

Not because I think I am better and I should always be mindful, but because I know how bad I feel when I am not. Although being mindful takes effort, I have never once regretted putting forth the effort.

"Try your best. That is all we can ask for."

This is what my parents told me from a very early age. That it was okay if I failed a test here and there, as long as I gave it my all. As long as I actually studied and really put the effort in, so long as I was mindful.

Even when I did fail a test, I wasn't upset with the grade, rather I was upset with myself, annoyed that I had not worked harder. Upset that I had chosen to spend my evening watching YouTube videos and procrastinating rather than studying.

Whenever you are mindful in life, you will never regret the things you do. Even when you fail, if you do it mindfully, you will be able to say that you tried your best and realize that you might need a little extra help or guidance. But if you spend your life in a mindless state, you will just keep kicking the can down the road, unable to receive the insights that life has to offer.

Everyone has problems.

This is not a radical statement. Everyone in the entire world has problems, no one is perfect, and therefore no one lives a problem-free life.

There are two ways to handle this fact:

1. Confront your problems head-on, with a willingness to learn and be attentive in the moment.
2. Ignore your problems; fill your life with distractions and kick the can down the road for as long as you can.

So yes, it is hard to be mindful at all times and there will be times when you realize how "mindless" you are being. But just like distractions in meditations, these moments of mindlessness are incredible, for they show us that we can do something, that we can make a change, that we can once again become mindful of our actions.

*"An unexamined life is not worth living."*

— SOCRATES

# CHAPTER 7

# GOING BEYOND
# THE BASICS

---

## FINDING A TEACHER

*"From the viewpoint of training in altruism, an enemy is really your guru, your teacher; only an enemy can teach you tolerance. An enemy is the greatest teacher of altruism, and for that reason, instead of hating, we must respect him."*

— HIS HOLINESS THE 14TH DALAI LAMA

This journey is not one that we should do alone. Often we will run into road blocks and challenges that require assistance. The good news is, we are not the first people to go down this path; we are not the first to sit down and look inside ourselves to see what is going on. This means we have teachers. We have access to so many people who have experience to offer.

Everyone in the world has teachers. Even the Dalai Lama, arguably one of the most advanced meditators in the world today, has teachers. There is so much merit to an individual who has made it his or her mission to teach others, there is a richness to this teaching and blocking this out would only hinder our personal advancement.

Anyone from the Buddha to a guy you meet on the street to your greatest enemy can be a teacher.

In the novel that jump-started my journey, *Way of the Peaceful Warrior* written by Dan Millman, Dan finds his teacher, Soc, in a gas station. This book, a novel that my father recommended I read, tells the story of Dan Millman, a college gymnast, who finds a spiritual teacher in the weirdest of circumstances. This experience changed his life and set him down a path of deep personal insight to find his ultimate meaning in the world. As I flipped through the pages, I knew that there was a reason I had been given this book, I felt like I was Dan, and I too would need to undergo my own personal discovery and find out who I was. After I turned the page to reveal the end of the book, I took two things from it:

1.  Find a random teacher at a gas station, which seemed highly unlikely and frankly pretty creepy.
2.  Meditate.

So that is what I did, I placed the book on my nightstand and sat at the foot of my bed ready to embark on my meditation journey.

**

Sitting in the pitch black I tried to clear my mind, but for the life of me, I could not seem to settle in, my mind kept racing. I was struggling to sit upright and drudging through the process of breathing.

Finally, I gave up thinking it must have been thirty minutes at this point. I remember feeling as if I had just gone through a grueling workout as I lay down to rest my back which was feeling strained from the time spent upright. Looking at my phone, it became clear that I had been sitting for only five minutes.

How could this be?

How could this thing that seemed so simple in explanation be so hard? I figured I just needed to try a little bit harder, so I sat back up and gave it another shot. Two minutes later

I gave up thinking it had been another ten minutes, feeling defeated I lay back down to rest. This happened repeatedly until I finally reached a total of twenty minutes of doing "meditation repetitions." I would sit and try to think about nothing for a few minutes, and then I would lay down for a much-needed break, almost as if I was in the gym.

Now this isn't everyone's experience with meditation. Some people struggle, some feel totally relaxed, some come away feeling great, others think that it was the worst few minutes of their lives. There is no exact way you are supposed to feel during or after a meditation but there are ways of making the process easier, of helping with the form per se and that is what teachers are for.

So what happened to my practice? Well I kept trying and for about two years I was a very inconsistent meditator, I would do it one morning and say, "This is awesome, I am going to do this every single day for the rest of my life." Then I would skip the next day because life happens and I couldn't seem to make the time and the next thing I knew it had been a month since my last meditation. But this did not have to be my fate, I did not have to struggle, trying to create this practice on my own without guidance. I treated this journey as if I was the first person to discover meditation, which is far from the truth; meditation has been around for thousands of years, with millions of practitioners and a wealth of knowledge waiting to be accessed. It wasn't until I started to find and utilize teachers that my practice solidified.

**

The traditional practice of finding a teacher takes six years.

Every teacher is different and has something unique to offer to students. One teacher may be best for me, but may not work for you. We all can understand this, as, throughout our time in school, we have had teachers who we really liked, who we felt like could really teach us. We have also had those who we have struggled to understand and whose class we couldn't wait to finish.

In Buddhist tradition, when one is looking for a teacher, they are asked to dedicate six years in order to affirm the relationship.

The first three years are for the student. The student spends this time observing the teacher, asking questions, trying to ascertain whether this individual would make a good guide. After this period, the student will ask for guidance.

Then it is the teacher's turn. He or she will spend the next three years observing the student, asking questions, trying to confirm that this individual will be a good student, one who will be able to listen and learn.

If the teacher is satisfied, then the student is accepted. If not, then the student must start again on the same process.

**

Could you imagine? Imagine if you dedicated six years in order to confirm that your 9th-grade math teacher was a right fit? Frankly, we would be in college by the time we found this individual and still be trying to learn algebra. Even later in life, we do not have this time; we do not have six years to dedicate solely to the practice of finding a meditation teacher. That is why we need to be willing to learn from anyone or anything, still questioning the information we receive but not blocking out anyone or anything as a potential teacher.

One of my first teachers was the Buddha; well the translated words of the Buddha that I found in a book, but nonetheless, I used pieces of the Buddha's teachings to anchor my practice. Teachers do not have to come in the traditional ways and as I look back now I realize that most of my original teachers were people I had never met. As a friend describes them, my teachers were "strangers whose names are so familiar on my bookshelf." Books were my first teacher, and they continue to be a wonderful guide on this journey, but they are not everything. There is so much to be learned from people face to face, people who can direct their words to your experience. These teachers can be both sought intentionally and randomly found.

As I started to amass my knowledge and work to find my way on this path, teachers started to reveal themselves. The first one was obvious. Two months after my first meditation, I had the opportunity to take an introduction to Buddhism class and as you may guess, my *teacher* became my first tangible guide.

I remember one time I sat down with her a few months into my meditation practice and she asked what my practice looked like. Describing the little space in my college dorm, in the corner of my room with a meditation pillow I bought off Amazon, I explained to her that I was struggling to find the drive to sit every day.

She looked at me and said, "How very western of you."

This brought me back, back to my studies. I thought back to the Buddha's teaching recognizing that one of the key pillars was the community, or Sangha in Sanskrit. I had isolated myself and my practice making it harder to flourish and grow. In my environment, finding a large meditation community that mimics a monastery in Asia is definitely hard, but I could build something similar. It was in this exchange that I realized the importance of finding teachers, the necessity to expand my practice beyond my tiny corner.

Everyone and everything can be a teacher if we open ourselves up to it, like how books, articles, movies and other things were a guide on my journey. However, as I said, and as many meditation "professionals" argue, there is merit to finding someone to interact with, someone to ask questions of, someone to keep you accountable and someone to help direct you on your journey.

These people can often help you in ways that nothing else could. They can be both a sounding board and an educational tool to open your eyes and show you a new perspective. Every teacher can help us be better teachers to ourselves, but we cannot do it alone, we cannot be all knowing and we never stop learning.

A few months ago, I was sitting with my friend Gregory Robison, the Executive Director of the Meditatio Foundation, an organization that offers academic courses, workplace programs, and tailored retreats in meditation for business leaders and professionals. We planned to speak about my capacity to create a meditation community at my college.

In a conversation that lasted an hour and a half, I remember talking about everything I had learned, how I had basically taught most of this to myself and how I had come so far from that initial two-minute meditation. I remember just continuing to talk thinking, "Wow this is going great. He can see how much I have accomplished in my young life."

As we wrapped up our conversation, Greg looked at me and asked if he could offer some advice. Eager to hear his comments, I leaned in to receive what I thought would be words of encouragement and praise on all that I had managed to do at such a young age. Instead, he looked me dead in the eye and said, "We have spoken for about an hour and a half, and in that time you have not asked me a single question. I am an interesting guy, I have lived all over the world, and I have a lot that I can offer."

In my desire to showcase myself, I completely lost my way, forgetting that the world is my teacher and the world was sitting right in front of me. When you think you are done learning, you are completely closed off to what life has to offer.

Sometimes the truth can sting. I built a persona around myself of being this mindful guy, one who was always open to the world wanting to constantly learn more and yet I spent that entire time closed off talking about only me, a person I already knew a lot about.

We can always learn, it doesn't matter from where or from whom. As long as we open ourselves up to the expansive world of knowledge around us, we will learn something.

When you are ready and willing to learn there will always be someone or something that can teach you. Even an experience like the one I just described, an experience where someone critiques you to your core, has lessons, sometimes the most important ones. This experience reminded me that the world is my teacher, and while I can also be a teacher to myself, it only impedes my journey to block off the world of knowledge. So I am not saying to go out and find a teacher in a gas station like Dan did in *Way of The Peaceful Warrior*, or talk about yourself to someone so he or she can point out your shortcomings. Rather, take a walk, sit in meditation, talk to a stranger, step out of your comfort zone, see what your world both internal and external has to offer.

## OPEN YOUR MIND

Life is about learning. Where I am sitting at this moment as a recent college graduate, I realize that the first 22 years of my life were dedicated to learning. I mean it is crazy when you think about it. From age 5 to 22 (for some people longer; others less), you spend pretty much every year in school, a systematic location for learning. Learning how to walk, learning how to talk, learning in school, learning in sports, learning in every aspect of my life, learning how to be a human being in this world and learning how to be myself; this was my life until now.

Now that my official career of learning is over, it feels a little bit like I am supposed to know everything and I should be ready for the "real world." However, this is far from the truth. Learning is simply part of the human experience; our brains are evolutionarily designed for it. All of our interactions provide the opportunity to learn more about ourselves, others, the world. As long as we remain open to the world around us, we can start to take in everything, to learn from everywhere and everyone.

In my final year of college, I took a class called Social Responsibility of Business. The class structure provided the opportunity simply to listen to the professor. With only a final paper and a few projects not fully related to the intricacies of the course instruction, I did not feel the need to take notes. Further given the lecture style format, there wasn't a huge demand for discussion, rather it was pure listening, pure learning.

I remember one class, in particular, I decided to go against my normal methods of note-taking. I kept my notebook, laptop, and phone all in my backpack and just sat there internalizing all of the information that the professor was presenting.

That hour and fifteen minutes flew by and as I stood up to leave, I realized that I retained so much more information than normal. To this day, more than eight months later, I can still tell you everything you would want to know about paid kidney donation all the way down to the stats and figures that were presented during class.

I can tell you that 8,000 people die in the United States every year waiting for a transplant. That the average price people are willing to pay for a kidney is around $40,000. That the only country in the world that has paid donation is Iran and they have a list of people looking to donate rather than a list of those in need. I learned and retained all of this information without ever taking a single note.

This experience showed me that the conventional way of learning might not always be best. School teaches us to take notes and memorize information to regurgitate later on tests. Often we fill our brain to the brim with the necessary facts, just to unload them after the exam, forgetting everything that we had learned. If I asked you to tell me something from 8th-grade history or 6th-grade science, you may remember one or two things that struck a chord, such as Eli Whitney invented the cotton gin or that an object in motion stays in motion unless acted upon by another force. But, I am willing to wager that most of the information has been washed down the drain, in one ear and out the other. This is how we have learned in school for years, feeling the necessity to memorize notes in order to pass exams rather than enjoying class and truly trying to learn the information.

Someone once told me, "We are never truly listening, simply just waiting to talk." This occurs in all facets of our life, not only school. Often in arguments with loved ones, we are thinking of a good come back, building up our ammunition so we don't lose the fight. We do this rather than try and truly listen to the words of someone we love. What if we listened, what if we actually tried to see what they were saying? Maybe the fight would end sooner, maybe we would realize they have a point as well and maybe our own anger or desire to have a side in the argument would dissipate, and there would be nothing left to argue.

When we meditate, we are listening, listening to what is going on within ourselves at this very moment. We aren't waiting to talk, to come up with some theory or some come-back. We aren't distracted by computers or phones. We aren't taking notes and missing that important piece of new information as we write down an old one. When we meditate, we are listening to our body, to our world both internal and external. This way when we get up from the cushion, we feel like we have learned something, we feel accomplished because this is raw learning: raw understanding unclouded by any distractions.

Even if it doesn't feel like you are learning from your practice, I promise you are.

I had the pleasure of interviewing Dr. Home H.C. Nguyen, the founder of MindKind Institute, an organization that works to teach the influencers of our world about the importance of being mindful.

Dr. Home teaches a six-week long mindfulness course. Sign up is voluntary and often the people who choose to partake in the course have an intrinsic desire to learn more about themselves and the techniques of mindfulness. But sometimes, individuals are encouraged to sign up by others in their lives. In this particular case, a course participant, who for the sake of the story will be called Eric, was encouraged to sign up by his girlfriend who was also taking the course. Eric was not at all thrilled to be learning mindfulness. He would sit there with a disgusted look on his face and his arms crossed, with practically zero desire to participate. During every session, there would be time for reflection, during which Eric would always pass. From a teacher's perspective, it seemed that Eric was miserable, closing himself off, resistant to learning anything and simply sitting through the material to please another person.

After about four weeks, and still no change, Dr. Home figured that there was nothing else he could do to help Eric.

He had been patient and had tried every angle to help this participant always coming from a place of love, and still nothing had worked. So Home decided that he would give Eric an out, tell Eric that he no longer needed to come, give Eric an opportunity to free himself from what seemed like torture.

On the Sunday night before the beginning of the fifth week of class, Dr. Home received an email.

Signing onto his computer Dr. Home looked to make sure there wasn't an emergency or a pressing concern from any of his students. Instead, he found a beautifully crafted email in his inbox signed from the one and only Eric.

The email explained how the course had changed Eric's life, it helped him realize all of the anger and latent emotion he had built up and how this blockage made him a difficult partner and person. Thankfully, after undergoing the course, Eric explained that he realized his shortcomings and was starting to see how he could become a better person, friend and boyfriend. He thanked Dr. Home for changing his life and said he was thoroughly looking forward to the remainder of the course.

Dr. Home did a double take, reading the email again and making sure he wasn't imagining this. He could not believe that even with all of the resistance, Eric was still learning, taking in the teachings around him until finally something clicked and Eric was able to truly open himself up to the world around him. This beautiful story shows that as humans we truly are always learning, even when we are resistant to the teachings, as long as we stick with it, something will click and we will continue to move forward in life. So when meditation gets hard and it feels like the practice is going nowhere just remember that you are always learning something.

**IMPORTANCE OF COMMUNITY**

Meditation is both an individual and collective journey.

It is a tale of a group of individuals pulling knowledge and practice from a universal collective. With this mindset, it would be a detriment to the practice simply to sit alone in a room.

Meditation since the time of the Buddha, always involved an aspect of community, a group of people working individually but also supporting one another at the same time. A community can help provide structure and hold each other accountable to the practice. Communities, or Sanghas in Sanskrit, like this are present all throughout Asia as there are thousands of monasteries with years of tradition and many followers.

Communities are also starting to flourish here in the West as Sanghas are popping up everywhere, whether they be small gatherings that meet weekly, or large groups that have a mission statement and a goal to bring meditation to the world. Regardless, meditation communities are as present as ever in the meditation generation.

Take MNDFL as an example. A meditation studio in New York City that was established by Lodro Rinzler. The premise is that for a small fee you reserve a pillow almost as if you were reserving a bike in a spin class. The point is that when you pay money, you feel accountable and are more likely to go. This studio is getting people in the door and helping to spread meditation in a world where it is hard to find the time.

This is just one example of the many Sanghas that are popping up in the 21$^{st}$ century. I am sure a Google search will reveal some even close to where you live. In my travels, I have discovered that there are communities all over the world, all striving toward the same collective goal, simply to build the practice and showcase its beauty and power.

\*\*

What if a Sangha isn't available to you? What if the meeting time doesn't work and what if no one your age is partaking in such things? Well the good news is that a community doesn't have a strict definition and even two people can form one.

Sharon Salzberg, one of the first practitioners to bring meditation to the West, explains how she and five friends have an email chain called "look left."

The originator of the chain found that when he got out of bed he could either turn right and head straight for his desk, or move left, directly to his meditation cushion. Thus a community was born. This simple email became their daily practice of reminding one another to meditate, with a nonjudgmental aura of simply sharing one's own practice, encouraging the others to do the same.

I have tried this same model with a few friends who want to start meditating regularly; I call them "friends of mind." I will simply send a text every morning after my daily meditation saying "breathe in." This text doesn't question or imply that they need to do their meditation in order to please me. Simply the aim is to remind that individual of the practice and reinforce the idea that they are not alone, that someone cares and wants them to benefit from a few minutes of meditation. This, I have found, is one of the best ways to start building a practice. It is also another example of how technology can help our practice, using phones and email to connect with "friends of mind" both far and near.

## MEDITATION AND TECHNOLOGY

Meditation is an old art form, one that was brought to the forefront of human existence during a time of less technology and fewer distractions. Meditation used to be much easier when humans were less distracted by the outside world and had the conditions to settle into silence. When the Buddha sat, he did not have to worry about missing out on some big event going on in the next town or fulfill himself by working some high paying job, and he definitely did not have to worry about how many likes his Instagram post was getting. The Buddha had conditions that allowed him to just sit and take in the world around and inside of him.

In today's environment, we do not have this same luxury. With the ubiquity of technology, we are facing a time full of distractions that pull us away from the present moment. In the time of the Buddha, if an event was going on and you didn't attend it was often because you had no idea of its existence. Now, information is available at our fingertips and usually, inability to attend an event is because you weren't invited. In this new technological age, we feel like we are always missing something, like what we are doing is never going to be as fun or as cool as what someone else is doing.

As the cell phone became more powerful and new platforms were developed, we now can see what other people are doing through Instagram and Snapchat. Often these snapshots and life snippets are overly optimistic and show a facade for how we are really feeling, portraying that we are always having the most fun and our life is incredible. Why do I say this? Because no one will ever post a Snapchat of themselves eating a dinner alone on a Friday night with nothing planned for the weekend ahead. Rather they would get some good lighting and post what looks like a home cooked meal with the caption, "Getting a good meal in for the night ahead."

Obviously, I am generalizing, but I do think that technology has become a huge distraction in our world, preventing us from being able to truly enjoy the moment. We are seeing everything through a screen rather than in real life. If you ever go to a concert, you can look around and witness a sea of phone lights, as people are recording the experience to post rather than just being there. We are constantly comparing ourselves to those we see on our little screen, and we often feel like what we are doing is not enough. As I said earlier, this is not a problem the Buddha had to deal with. He never needed to Instagram his journey to enlightenment or worry that his hair (or lack thereof) may look bad to his Snapchat followers.

**

It is not all bad, technology has also done some incredible things. Technology has allowed us to connect to the world.

Before our circle was only as wide as our feet could walk and our mouths could talk. Now, we can reach friends on the other side of the planet with just a few taps of our thumbs. It is such a powerful tool that can help us in so many ways, as long as we use it as an aid rather than a distraction.

Lodro Rinzler told me a story about two individuals that walked into a MNDFL studio in New York. They were friends, who wanted to do a little meditation amidst a crazy day.

What Lodro came to find out was that these two individuals had just met in person for the first time. Now I know what you might be thinking and no, this was not a Tinder date. Rather, these two individuals met on Insight Timer, a meditation app that provides everything from your basic timer to recorded guided meditations. The app also has this feature where it will show you other users meditating at the same time as you. This feature fosters a sense of community, reminding an individual that while they may be sitting alone in this moment, there are so many other people on this journey with you.

It turns out that the two individuals who walked into MNDFL that afternoon met using this feature. After several weeks, they realized that they were both meditating at the same time every day. They did not live anywhere near each other. One lived in New York, while the other lived all the way on the other side of the Atlantic Ocean in Norway. Yet they felt connected. After they noticed this mutual meditation time, they started talking and eventually became friends and meditation buddies. That is why they walked into MNDFL, in order to do their daily meditation.

This is the power of technology. It allowed these two individuals to connect from thousands of miles away. It allowed them to build their meditation practices together; it created a sense of community, a virtual meditation sangha.

Technology has the power to bridge a gap that meditation has faced for years. Before this practice could only reach those in dire need, those willing to travel the distance to hear the teaching, and those who were born into it and grew up with the knowledge. Now meditation can be accessed by anyone at any time.

Headspace, another meditation app on the market, has a ten-day introduction course taught by founder Andy Puddicombe. Andy spent ten years of his life as a monk and is now using this app to teach meditation to as wide an audience as possible. He uses modern analogies and animations in order to present this material in a way that everyone can understand.

Technology can help us learn, spread, and access meditation on a whole new level, we just need to know how to use it as an aid, rather than a distraction.

CHAPTER 8

# ADDING TOOLS TO THE TOOLKIT

———

This chapter is broken into two main parts:

1.  Mindful Practices: times throughout your day where it is great to employ mindfulness techniques.
2.  Other Practices: other practices that are akin to meditation and mindfulness. They are not exactly meditation or mindfulness, but they are in the family and can really enhance the central practice.

## MINDFUL WALKING

It may seem a little strange to take time out of your day to purposely walk at the pace of a snail. It would be even weirder if you were doing this in public with people watching you walk and thinking maybe there was something wrong with your legs. Luckily walking meditation can be amended slightly in order to apply it to everyday life.

This is a practice I have borrowed from Chade-Meng Tan, author of *Search Inside Yourself*. He talks about applying walking meditation in the office, using a practice of paying attention to your walk even if it is just from your desk chair to the bathroom.

I was very intrigued when I read this idea in Meng's book. I thought about all the times I walk throughout the day. Whether it is the initial walk from my bed to brush my teeth and get ready for the day or the walk from my house to class or to work or, even as Meng presented, the several trips a day to the bathroom. So unless you live within arms distance of the bed, the bathroom and the kitchen, it is safe to assume that you have to walk somewhere throughout the day.

Thinking back on my life and even just on my day, I started to realize that often when I am walking somewhere it is always about the destination and not the journey. I am so set on getting to my end goal that I often cannot remember anything special from the walk. I tend to blur out my surroundings, unable to take in the scenery or the people, unable to interact with the world around me. If I have to walk anyway, why tune out the world and just focus on where I am going, why not embrace what is around me in that moment and find joy in the process itself?

It reminded me of Sisyphus, a mythological character who was cursed by the gods to spend all of eternity pushing a rock up a hill. Once he got to the top of the hill, the rock would roll all the way back down, and he would have to return to the bottom and start again. Over and over again he would be forced to do this, never reaching his destination. However, much to the gods' disappointment, Sisyphus started to enjoy his punishment. He enjoyed the process of pushing the rock and was actually disappointed when he got to the top. He started to enjoy the journey.

Luckily, none of us (I would hope) are forced to push a big rock up a steep hill, but the lesson is still extremely applicable. If we start to enjoy the journey, we could increase our overall enjoyment and still make it to our destination.

**Putting the practice to action:**

- To extrapolate the practice of walking meditation into real life, our goal is simply to pay attention to the sensations and feelings of walking as we do it.
- For example: if you are in class or at the office and need to go to the bathroom, don't just get up and start mindlessly walking

towards your destination. Instead, try making the moment extremely important. Focus on the act of standing up or the initial push off to go somewhere else.

- As you start to walk feel the contact of your feet with the ground. Notice how different surfaces provide a different sensation to the bottom of your foot (even while you are wearing shoes). Feel the activation of your muscles as they start to engage in the act of walking.

- Try to focus on your breathing as well throughout this process, seeing how it feels to just be in the moment, doing nothing but the simple act of walking, an act that for the first few years of our lives we struggled to perfect, constantly falling down unable to go where we wanted. And now, we walk anywhere we want without any effort.

- Try to pay attention, maybe not to all of these feelings and sensations at once, but simply see what it feels like to walk with a focused mind.

## MINDFUL EATING

This right here is one of the hardest exercises that you will read about in this book. Who would guess that something we do practically 3 times a day, every day could actually be so hard, yet everyone I know has really struggled with this practice, including me. Often meal times can seem forced. Eating can seem like something we have to do rather than something we enjoy. Eating can also be a coping mechanism or an activity that produces a lot of anxiety. According to the National Eating Disorder Association, at least 30 million people in the United States suffer from an eating disorder. That is almost 10% of the population, and I am sure that there are even more people who just have some difficulties surrounding food but wouldn't classify it as a disorder.[11]

We spend a lot of our time mindlessly eating. Picture the large tub of popcorn at the movie theater. Whenever I go see a movie, that thing is half full before the commercials are over. This is often something with which we are all familiar, maybe it isn't the popcorn example, but the idea of opening a snack and eating the entire bag without even noticing, just shoveling handful after handful into our mouths. This is what I call mindless eating, eating without paying attention to what you are doing. Well, in mindful eating, we try and do the exact opposite.

Mindful Eating:

- The practice of mindful eating is simple but as you can probably guess by now, not easy. It requires us to pay attention to each bite of food as we eat.
- Choose a meal, preferably one where you are alone. This will prevent you from needing to make conversation during the

11 "What Are Eating Disorders?" 2018. *National Eating Disorders Association.*

exercise and allow you to focus just on the food. In line with this idea, you will want to shut off your phone, computer, TV and any other distractions.

- The process of mindful eating starts before the first bite. Make sure that your hands are washed and that your area is prepped and ready for the meal. This will make the experience special as we rarely put much preparation into the process of actually eating our food.

- Sit down in front of the plate and stare at your food for a moment. Think about all of the effort that went into making the food, all of the individuals including you who had a hand in preparing this beautiful meal right in front of you. Say a small thank you to all of those people giving gratitude for the ability to fill your stomach with food.

- Next smell the food, notice what sensations surround this action. Does your mouth start to water, does your stomach grumble. What does it feel like to draw out the process before actually eating the food?

- Finally take your first bite. Make sure that it is a regular size bite and that the food isn't too hot or too cold. Chew the food slowly, really trying to savor every flavor that is encompassed in the bite. Make sure that you finish the first bite before putting the next one in.

- Try and do this for the entirety of the meal and see how it feels. Take a pause between each bite and really try to gauge if you are still hungry. Often we eat more than we need because we are eating so fast, our brain doesn't have time to register that the stomach is full. So be mindful throughout the entire meal.

This is often a difficult exercise as most of us are used to eating very quickly or at least having some sort of company even in the form of our phones or computers while we eat. However, the objective of this process is to try and change our relationship with food. To make eating an action that provides nothing but pure enjoyment. This is fueled by both savoring and giving purpose to each bite. Also the slowed down speed of eating helps us to eat only what our body needs without over-indulging. Often we tend to eat beyond what our body needs because our stomach has not had the time to process and send the signal to the brain that we are full. By slowing down and giving time to each bite, we can eat just the right amount.

My friend told me about another exercise that also might be interesting to try as a preparation for doing a full session of mindful eating. She detailed how her teacher handed out raisins to everyone in the class. The teacher asked the students to look at the raisin, smell the raisin, and finally slowly put the raisin into their mouths. The teacher then asked them to keep the raisin in their mouths for 15 minutes without chewing. They were asked to pay attention to the texture, to the flavor seeing how it changed over time.

I have also tried this exercise with a piece of candy, a little gummy candy that I would normally just chew up right away and move on to the next piece, fueling my sugar addiction. But after I heard about this exercise I figured I would see what it felt like to try and fully experience the piece of food in my mouth. To make it even more fun, I decided to make it a competition between me, my friend and my brother to see who could keep the piece of candy in their mouths the longest without chewing.

15 Minute Food:

- Pick a small piece of food, something like a raisin, or a gummy candy.
- Put the piece of food in your hand and observe it, turn it over and see every inch, every detail that surrounds the item.
- Slowly place it into your mouth and hold it there. Notice the textures as you push it around your mouth with your tongue. Notice the flavors and how they change as the food stays in your mouth for a longer period.
- Try to keep your focus on the piece of food throughout the entire process.
- Finally, after the 15 minutes are up—or when you are ready to lose the competition against your friends—chew the piece of food. Enjoy the process of chewing, think of it as a reward for all of your hard work, all of the effort you put into keeping the food in your mouth for so long.

I am a very competitive person and so is my friend so obviously, we spent close to 30 minutes at a bar with just a single piece of candy in our mouths. The competition went on for so long that by the end of it, both of our candies had dissolved into practically nothing. Unfortunately, for me, he did manage to win the competition, but we all learned more about giving time and care to the food that we put into our bodies.

## MINDFUL DRINKING

Given the context of this book, I wanted to tackle this interesting conversation of mindful drinking. Is it possible to drink while still remaining mindful, while still paying attention in the present moment? Drinking has become a phenomenon on college campuses. Not only is it socially acceptable to drink to the point of memory loss and physical impairment, this act can sometimes feel like a requirement.

I remember walking into my first college pregame. Entering the threshold of the small freshman dorm room, I could feel the change in temperature. They tried to sandwich as many young, eager 18-year-olds, as possible into a room no bigger than 200 square feet. From my count, they managed to get 20 people. Aside from the heat and the smell of sweat, the thing I remember most was the pressure to drink. I don't mean peer pressure, because frankly I was also an eager freshman and was looking forward to having a few drinks without having to hide the alcohol from my parents. The pressure came from the need to drink a lot and quickly.

"Hurry, take as many shots as you can, because we need to leave soon and there won't be enough alcohol at the next party!" This was the prognosis of the dorm's inhabitant, reminding all of us to drink as much as we could so we could be nice and drunk by the time we left. Obviously, I wanted to fit in, so I figured that this individual knew their stuff and I listened, taking as many shots as I could in the short time I was allotted.

I paid the price the next morning, unable to get out of bed because my pounding headache would not leave me alone. My memory of the night before was hazy and I just wanted to sleep until infinity.

Much of my college career, was a rinse and repeat of the process above, thinking that I had no other way, no other way to go out and have fun. I figured that I needed to pound drinks in order to have a good time and in order to make friends.

**

Drinking would often conflict with my meditation practice. For most of the week, I would be mindful, trying to meditate every day and trying to enjoy and live in the present moment; then the weekends would come and I would drink to the point of numbness. I tried to avoid the deeper feelings within me, hoping that when I found the bottom of the bottle my troubles would go away. Instead, I just found a lot of headaches, pain and occasionally an early morning waking up on a sidewalk. My drinking habits would constantly take me out of the present moment, take me out of my own mind, impairing my ability to live in the here and now. On top of this, my drinking was dangerous. I was hurting myself and the people closest to me, but I did not see another choice. I felt like in order to be cool, in order to make it through college, I needed to drink.

It is not just me. Binge drinking has become a huge problem in college and beyond. According to one study, in the U.S., children ages 12–20 account for 11% of the total alcohol consumed. Further, 90% of this alcohol is consumed in the form of binge drinking, meaning the consumption of five or more drinks in one sitting. Binge drinking does not stop even once you are of age, studies show that 25.7% of people ages 25–34 binge multiple times a month.[12]

This does not have to be your fate. There is indeed a way to drink while still being mindful. Lodro Rinzler, the author of *The Buddha Walks into a Bar* and Co-Founder of MNDFL,

---

12 "Fact Sheets – Binge Drinking." 2018. *Centers For Disease Control And Prevention.*

has an excellent take on how this is done. It is not drinking that is the issue rather it is the intoxication. Drinking itself is not a harm, frankly, studies are now saying that a glass of red wine a day may have some excellent health benefits.[13] The issue comes from alcohol intoxicating you, meaning that it causes you to lose power over your behavior. Mindful drinking aims at preventing this.

In order to drink mindfully, you need to drink. In order to analyze our relationship with something, we need to first have one. So if you don't drink, I do not want you to start in order to do this practice. But if you do drink, then this practice is great to try the next time you have a few.

Mindful Drinking:

- Next time you are out grabbing a drink or reaching for a beer out of the fridge try this practice.
- Before you open or pour yourself a drink, ask yourself, why am I drinking? If you are satisfied with the answer you produce than pour away. But if you start to doubt your justification— perhaps you are avoiding something or trying to suppress certain feelings—then maybe you should hold off and consider whether drinking will actually help.

---

13 The Mayo Clinic. 2016. "Red wine and resveratrol: Good for your heart?" *The Mayo Clinic.*

- As you take that first sip, focus on the flavors. Do you actually like the drink? Or are you drinking it for another reason?
- How does the drink make you feel? Maybe it relaxes you, maybe it loosens some tension in your body. Whatever it is sit with that feeling.
- When you finish the drink, ask yourself if you want another one. There is nothing wrong with having a few drinks, but see if you want one or if you need one. Do you have power over your choice, or is the alcohol becoming a crutch?
- Try to keep track of these feelings as you start to drink more, monitoring where you are mentally and physically. If you start to feel drunk, ask yourself if this is a feeling you were looking for. Did you want to be drunk? What is it about being drunk that you enjoy?
- If you are like me and don't actually enjoy drinking, now would be a good time to think about what else could give you the feeling that alcohol is providing. For instance, if you need to feel more relaxed, could you take a nice warm bath rather than drinking a few glasses of wine?

This practice is not one that can be done immediately, but if you do want to change your relationship with drinking, I would suggest giving this a try. You may find that you are much happier going out having a drink or two and being able to wake up the next day without a headache, or you may find that you don't like drinking at all. Regardless of what you find, the hope is that this practice will allow you to have control over your relationship with alcohol, not the other way around.

I have done this practice myself. After many nights of drinks and even more mornings of headaches and apologies, I realized that I needed to reassess my relationship with alcohol. I realized that drinking allowed me to avoid my problems, to kick the can down the road a little longer. When I would drink, I would forget everything that I needed to deal with, like the worries of graduating college and getting a job or feeling even bigger issues like I wasn't a good enough person. It wasn't until I took a deeper look at my habits that I realized these things, I realized that the drinking was a front for a much bigger issue.

As I started to deal with these issues, I realized that I no longer felt like I needed to drink. Alcohol no longer had any power over me, and I was free to choose whether or not I wanted to drink.

## MINDFUL ROUTINES

Even though I do not drink anymore, I am still a big coffee fanatic. Unlike most college students who start drinking coffee in order to cope with the long hours of studying and partying, I started drinking coffee at a very early age. When people ask why, I explain to them that I am part Italian and that my Dad is a big espresso drinker. The part that I don't usually explain is it is my mother who is Italian and my father has no ties to Italian culture other than his love for espresso, pasta, and pizza.

Regardless, when I was younger my dad used to always tell me, "Coffee is the lifeblood." To be honest I never knew what it meant but for some reason, I just started to believe that coffee was the key to life. What I really think happened here was that my dad reached what I call the "sharing phase" of caffeination. It is where you are so jacked up on caffeine that you want someone else to know and/or join you in this experience. So, this is how my journey to loving coffee began, with a straight espresso shot at the age of 12. From there it looked a little bit like the transition of Will Ferrell's character in *Kicking and Screaming,* going from never having coffee, to now yelling at other people that "Coffee is the lifeblood that fuels the dreams of champions."

Do not worry if you do not drink coffee, this is not a section that requires you to start fueling an addiction to caffeine, rather I want to discuss morning routines. Every morning when I wake up I have a routine that I very much enjoy. It involves a nice morning shower to wake me up, a meditation session and then a cup of whatever coffee I feel like making that day. I have had this routine for months now, and I am very happy when I accomplish everything on this list.

However, there is one problem, when I do not follow this routine I am often annoyed with myself, I am often angry that I have not checked off the items on my list.

I am sure you have a morning routine yourself, whether it is just waking up at the last minute and running to your first meeting or to class, or if you have a more drawn out routine that requires you to wake up early. Whatever your routine is, I am sure it feels pretty bad when you do not stick to it, when we sleep through class or wake up too late to get through our checklist. This is something that everyone deals with. The goal here is to try and overcome the negative sentiment around "ruining" your routine and rather finding ways to still enjoy your mornings even when you do not accomplish everything on your checklist.

Putting practice into action:

- When you wake up in the morning what is your checklist, what do you need to do before you leave the house? Try to think about this routine. Think about what it feels like when you accomplish everything on this list, when you leave for the day having done everything you wanted to do that morning.
- Now think about what it would feel like or does not feel like to accomplish this list, to wake up too late, or blow off the checklist for other distractions, like watching TV, rather than making breakfast for ourselves.

- Try to transform these negative feelings, rather than thinking you have woken up too late and could possibly not accomplish your routine, try to think about what you can do in the time that you have remaining. If you want to meditate for 5 minutes every morning but you woke up too late, do you have time for 1 minute, for 30 seconds?
- Rather than being upset with what has already occurred, you can feel a sense of pride with having thought through a difficult situation, for having had less time than usual and still accomplishing some of the things you wanted to do that morning. It doesn't have to be an all-or-nothing mentality, rather we can still make the time for what is important.

With this practice, we are simply trying to change our view from negative to positive. So instead of getting down on ourselves when we fail to wake up at the time we want or are unable to achieve everything we have lined up for ourselves that morning, we can feel proud about our ability to react in the moment to the situation at hand and still accomplish a lot. In this way, we can react without negativity, with kindness and compassion for ourselves, with the understanding that what we really needed that day was a little extra sleep.

Once we increase our comfortability with being able to change and adjust our routines, we can start to make them even more special. Often when things become too routine, they are not nearly as enjoyable. We get sucked into the habitual action and all of a sudden things we loved to do that gave us a sense of pride, like making breakfast in the morning or meditating, start to become burdensome. Our checklist becomes a chore rather than a pleasure. Luckily, this does not have to be our fate, there are ways to make routines fresh and exciting to help avoid that feeling of failure while also keeping the joy of the action.

Making the morning coffee:

- Take an activity that has become so habitual that it no longer provides any source of enjoyment and is rather a chore that you need to do. For the purposes of this example, I will use the act of making morning coffee.
- Walking into the kitchen (or wherever you would make your coffee), think about the end goal here, to put something into your body that not only will help wake you up but that should also provide an enjoyable taste (even if that means adding sugar and milk).
- Begin the process of making the cup, doing everything as if it were for the first time. Truly immerse yourself in the action trying to use what is in front of you to make the perfect cup of coffee.
- Get the water to the right temperature, get the right amount of coffee grinds, and add the perfect amount of milk and sugar. Get the coffee to be to your liking whatever that may be.

- Bring the coffee back to your desk or wherever you are planning to enjoy it. Make sure you wait until it cools down rather than rushing right in, that way you don't burn your mouth.
- Finally, take a sip as if you are tasting the drink for the first time. See how it tastes, see if you notice a difference, if you can taste the effort that went into making it just the way you like it. If you are using coffee pods or are ordering the coffee from somewhere else, think about all of the effort and people it took to get you your coffee.
- What does it feel like to savor something as if you are doing it for the first time? Try and apply this mentality to all of the things you do whether it is the taste of the minty toothpaste, or the effort of getting your outfit just right in the morning or even making the bed.

With this exercise, you will hopefully begin to find more joy in the activities that have started to become more routine. And if you still don't enjoy the activity, it might mean it's time for a change. Don't worry I am not saying you need to stop drinking coffee, or start, but maybe you change the type of coffee you drink… maybe you explore until you find the perfect cup for you. You should enjoy your routine actions that is why they are part of your routine. So put the effort into making it exciting, not just a boring old routine—you should want to get up and do it!

## MINDFUL DISHES

If we can stop our routine from feeling like a chore, maybe we can do the same with our real chores.

Everyone hates doing dishes.

It could easily be the worst chore in the modern world. Actually, on a bunch of blogs and chat rooms, it is considered the worst, non-bathroom related household chore. Gosh, the thought of walking back into my house to see a sink full of dirty dishes, makes me cringe. For me, it was even worse in college before I had a dishwasher and needed to wash everything by hand.

I remember one day, my friend Evan came over. We cooked a nice big meal, using pretty much every dish that I had in my apartment. Since I did most of the cooking, Evan volunteered to take care of the dishes. I was grateful and I sprawled on the couch to watch Evan work. He was moving as fast as he could, with the water so hot that he was basically burning his hands with every dish. Seeing this, I thought about how often I did the same, how often I took an activity that already sucked and made it worse, by having the water be so uncomfortably hot, and trying to rush through it.

We all like the feeling of taking a nice warm bath or stepping into a nice warm hot tub. Why not try to get the same feeling from washing dishes? Even though we are not going to submerge ourselves in the kitchen sink, we can still spend the few seconds to get the water temperature to a comfortable level, one that we actually enjoy putting our hands in. Instead of having to wash the dishes, why can't we look at this chore as "taking a bath with your dishes?"

Taking a Bath with Your Dishes:

- Next time you have to wash dishes, try this practice. Start by getting the water temperature to a comfortable level, adjusting it as if you were filling a tub to take a bath. I don't care how long it takes, don't start washing until the water is just right.
- Take the first dish and run it under the water. As you begin to clean it, try and focus on the sensations, the feeling of the water on your skin, the weight of the dish in your hand. Like all of these meditation practices, try to be in the present moment, just focusing on washing the dish.
- Continue to do this with every dish until the sink is empty. Make this process important, take pride in the work you are doing even if it is just a simple household chore.

Now every time Evan comes over, we have an argument over who gets the privilege of doing the dishes. Imagine that, two college-age boys fighting over who gets to wash the dirty dishes. Both of us have learned to love the process even if the action itself is not that fun and we have started to pride ourselves on being able to keep a smile while doing chores.

Even though washing dishes is not the ideal way to spend a Saturday afternoon, it does not need to be a chore that we hate. Rather through this practice, we can learn to love even the worst of chores and tasks. You can try this with activities like folding laundry, mowing the lawn, taking out the trash; whatever you are doing, when you pay attention to the present moment, you learn to find more enjoyment in the little details of the task.

**

## BUILDING YOUR MEDITATION SPACE

I have a friend who was interested in learning meditation, saying that it might help her with anxiety. So just as I have done in the beginning of this book, I explained why meditation is helpful and how to use various practices to help achieve your desired goals, your motivations.

After a quick five minute session, she expressed great enjoyment of the practice. As we got up from the pillows to continue talking, she asked me, "So where did you get these pillows? Are these the best pillows for meditation? Is there certain clothing that I should wear while meditating?"

I burst out laughing.

"Try the practice a few more times before going on an Amazon shopping spree to decorate yourself as a meditator," I responded.

Obviously, she responded with, "The pillows and the outfits will help me to build the practice, once I have those things then I can really start!"

In many activities that we want to start, it often feels like we are getting part of the way there just by buying the necessary equipment. So if we want to start doing yoga we might buy a mat or some clothes; if we want to start playing an instrument we might buy a guitar or a keyboard. Sometimes it feels like we have made progress when we are outfitted for the role, but actually playing the role is much harder.

Even for me, I bought meditation cushions probably after my third time meditating, thinking that once I made the investment, the practice would definitely follow. Of course, I spent almost a year owning meditation cushions before I actually started to put them to good use. Before that, they were just decorations, collecting dust in the corner of my room.

One of my teachers, Joan, told me about the invention of the Tibetan singing bowl. You know those round metal bowls with a wooden mallet that is used to produce a singing noise as you trace the mallet around the bowl (if you do not know what I am talking about, a quick Google search will help with that, producing that "oooh, yes I know what you are talking about" feeling).

Well Joan said that these bowls were invented by gift shop owners who realized that they could attach the word Tibetan to it and say that the bowls are used in meditation. Lo and behold, the purchase of these items skyrocketed. I am willing to bet that many people interested in meditation have one and think that it is integral to the act of meditation, buying it for its long spiritual tie to the Tibetan monk community. Well, think again. Don't worry though, I am the proud owner of one myself, and it serves as a great decoration in my meditation space.

We like things. It has become part of human nature to feel a sense of satisfaction when we own things, and we are way more willing to spend money on things that we believe make us better at our hobby. So, it is only natural to want to buy the Tibetan singing bowl or the meditation cushion in order to help make your practice tangible. Well for once in this book, I am not going to tell you that you are doing something wrong or need to do something different. Buying these items is totally okay and can, in fact, be beneficial if you put them to good use.

Another one of my teachers, Kieran, talked about the importance of building your meditation space. About trying to define a particular space for your practice and making it yours. Obviously, on the surface, this would seem counter-intuitive to imagine that an activity that requires you to sit and try to get some separation from material possessions would actually be positively influenced by these things, but in building out your space you help build your practice. This is why buying some items that excite and entice you to meditate is not the worst thing in the world.

As many of us probably know it is easy to try something once. Most of us are willing to or already have given meditation a try, the hard part is continuing to practice after that initial introduction. In order to make the practice feel more real to you, to help you continue in the face of life's adversity, which doesn't always allow for new hobbies, it is important to add this element of individuality to the practice, making it something you personally take pride in.

This is why we decorate our meditation area. Whether it be cushions to help with posture or pictures of those we love to help with motivation, designing the space helps us continue this practice even when life gets in the way. The goal here is to create a space that you walk into and your brain immediately starts to think: meditation time.

Putting the practice into action:

- Pick a space in your house, your dorm room, your apartment or wherever you live, and set that aside to be your meditation space, a space used only for meditation. It doesn't have to be a separate room, it can simply be the corner of a room or a closet dedicated to meditation.
- The idea is to create a space where the sight of it sends a signal to the brain to sit and meditate, kind of like the time-old psychology experiment of Pavlov's dog.[14] In line with this idea, do not choose your meditation space to be your bed as your brain will think about sleep the second you get into the bed.
- Once you have the space, decorate it first with things that fuel your motivation. Whether it is pictures of family members or letters to yourself or your journal place it in the space as a reminder of why you are starting this practice. It can even be a piece of paper you write on during this exercise that has a motivation written on it. Or you can think back to the example you thought of in Chapter One of when you were recently most happy, and try and embody this thought within the space.
- Outfitting the room with candles and other scents is also a great idea. Our brains are filled with associations triggered

---

14 Ivan Pavlov was a Russian psychologist who was well known for his work in the field of classical conditioning. He used dogs to demonstrate that a stimulus (for instance a bell) that would not produce any response from the dog on its own, but when paired with the reward of food, the bell can cause the dog to salivate. This study showed that we can create natural responses using stimuli.

by our senses. We are already playing with sight by adding images and other objects, but we can also use scent as a trigger for meditation so that when you smell lavender, or whatever scents you choose, you brain will immediately think of meditation.

- (Optional): If you are the type of person that likes to buy all of the necessary activity essentials before beginning the activity, here is the place to do it. While I do not recommend spending money right away, it can be helpful to find, borrow, or even purchase cushions or a tapestry or anything else that can help make the meditation space feel like it is yours, a space that you are excited to come to every day.

## JOURNALING

Often when we meditate, things come to the surface of our mind that we often are trying to ignore. For example, if you are anxious about a big exam or a presentation at work, you will most likely experience that anxiety during the meditation. Now as I have explained earlier in the book, there is nothing wrong with anxiety, for our goal is just to observe whatever is here right now in the moment. So if anxiety is present, let it be present. However, this is often not a very helpful diagnosis and leaves people wanting more. Often people meditate because they want to get rid of anxiety and they are frequently disappointed when the anxiety tends to creep up especially when it happens during the meditation. This is when people will usually say that meditation just isn't for them and that it isn't helping them, but it isn't so much a problem with meditation as it is a problem with expectations. Meditation is aimed at generating a greater ability to place oneself in the present moment whatever that moment may be, allowing you to cope with difficult feelings, like anxiety, rather than trying to make them go away.

You should not expect meditation to magically solve all of your problems. Rather, by building up our ability to live in the present moment, becoming comfortable with whatever thoughts or feelings we are having in that moment, trying not to cast judgement over our mental state, we can slowly start to reduce anxiety, feel a greater sense of calm, and develop more contentment with our lives. However, sometimes we need a quicker fix, sometimes our feelings are so strong that we simply cannot sit through them. When this happens, it can often create an adverse relationship with meditation, making it an activity that is mentally connected to these strong negative feelings, which in turn makes it hard for us to find the desire to meditate.

This is where journaling comes in. Journaling can help us to deal with some of the emotions and feelings we are experiencing right now. Using a stream of consciousness style of writing, we can put our thoughts to paper. By seeing our thoughts right there in front of us, they tend to carry less weight, to not hold as much power over us.

## Meditation Journaling:

- This practice should be done when we are struggling to meditate, whether it is an inability to focus during a meditation, a continuous reoccurring thought during our sits or an adverse feeling towards the practice.
- Open up a journal or simply get out a piece of paper and start by writing a prompt at the top of the page. Here are but a few examples:
  - Meditation thoughts…
  - My struggle to sit is coming from…
  - I dislike meditating because…
  - I would rather be doing…
- I have found that writing the prompt can help me start the process for I have already started writing, making the task seem less daunting. It also provides some much needed guidance and structure.
- Once the prompt is in front of you, take a 2–3 minutes to sit and think about the prompt. What are the initial thoughts that come to mind? How do the thoughts change over these few minutes?
- Now you can begin to write. This is stream of consciousness writing—meaning that you are simply writing whatever you are feeling in the moment even if that means writing sentence

fragments or half sentences as new thoughts start to pop into your head. (No one is reading this besides you. The goal is simply to get what is inside your head onto the paper).

- Try to write for 5–8 minutes straight, or if you prefer, until you reach the end of the page. Try not to move the pen from the paper. If you run out of things to write, simply write "I have nothing to say" over and over again until you once again have things to say.

- Once you finish the exercise, read what you wrote. This is one of the more difficult parts of this task as it is often scary to read what we are feeling, but reading it helps us better understand our own emotions as we can now see the discomfort we didn't want to or couldn't think about. This is key to decreasing the power our emotions hold over us.

- No one is making you hold on to these words. So if you desire, you can throw it out, rip it up, burn it, do whatever feels right. The purpose is to just get these thoughts out and see them in real life in front of your eyes. Once that is done, the choice is yours!

This exercise of meditation journaling should help in the moment, helping to aid our ability to sit day after day, allowing us to overcome the obstacles and hurdles that might present themselves as we start to build the practice.

Journaling should not stop here though. We do not need to journal only when dealing with difficult emotions. Rather, journaling can be a preventative exercise. By journaling every day, we can build a deeper understanding of ourselves, allowing us to notice when emotions start to become overwhelming before they totally consume our ability to do things like meditate.

A daily journaling practice is a great thing to start, and unlike meditation, it is tangible. You can see the pages start to build up as you continue to write and this is often very satisfying.

Creating a daily journaling practice:

- Much like the meditation journaling exercise, we will start with a prompt. I have provided a short list of those later in the chapter, but really the prompt can be anything that will help spark our writing. It can often be daunting to open up the book to a blank page and start writing, so a prompt can often serve as a guide.
- Think about your prompt for a few minutes (2–3 minutes) just letting your brain play with the question at hand.
- Afterward set a timer or determine a page count and begin writing. Try to keep your pen to the paper the entire time using the filler sentence "I have nothing to say" when you run out of answers.
  - Also, try your best not to use the eraser or cross stuff out. This might be hard as it can feel tempting to want to correct our work, but in this exercise, you want to just see

what flows. If you write something wrong, just go with it and see where it takes you, you never know where it could lead.

- Look over what you have written allowing your visual thoughts to sink in and end by thanking yourself for putting in the effort to try and better understand who you are.

This practice done daily can really help one get comfortable in their own skin, in their own environment, continuously trying to understand themselves through constructive writing. I can personally attest to this as I do this practice every day finding that it helps me to put the whirlwind of my thoughts onto paper allowing me to gain greater clarity and calmness in both my life and especially within my meditation practice. For me, journaling is a predecessor to a good meditation, allowing me to untangle my thoughts before sitting and trying to be with whatever is there.

When I started this practice, I found it very helpful to have prompts written out in advance. Since then I have created what I call a journal jar. It is a little mason jar that has a bunch of small pieces of paper, each with its own journaling prompt on it. This way every time I sit down to journal, I can reach my hand into the jar and pull out a prompt to help me start my practice. It is also a fun activity almost as if I am pulling out a surprise present every time I reach my hand into the jar. Simply the suspense of not knowing the prompt makes it all the more fun. I encourage you to make your own journal jar and much like building our meditation space, have fun with this activity by making the jar specific to you. Either by using colors you like or putting some motivating pictures or quotes inside of the jar to help you keep up the practice.

The journal jar is definitely not for everybody. Some people would prefer to just write without a prompt, some people might even prefer to draw. This is all totally fine! There are no rules in this exercise other than just trying to create a greater understanding of yourself so if opening the page and letting the pen fly is your style, by all means, go and do that. Eventually, the pages will fill up and then the books and then the bookshelf and you will have a collection of your journals, an encyclopedia of yourself that you created. I have a mentor who is on journal volume 109, would you believe that! Let's say the average journal has 100 sheets or 200 pages front and back. That means that my mentor has written over 21,000 pages about his life, his journey. He has created something tangible that tells his story, a story that he can pass on to his children, that is incredible. That could be us one day if we stick with this practice.

For now, here are some initial journaling prompts:

- Right now I am feeling…
- I am thankful for…
- I am inspired by…
- Something I want to say to my past (future) self is…
- What kindness can I offer myself right now…
- I really wish others knew this about me…
- The words I'd like to live by are…
- What brings tears to my eyes is…
- Love is…

## HUMAN BEINGS VS. HUMAN DOINGS

I recently got back from a meditation retreat in Nepal. Like most retreats or events where new people gather together, we were asked to introduce ourselves providing our general information like your name and where you are from, and then, of course, we had to answer the harder question of why we were here, why we traveled all the way to Nepal for a meditation retreat? This is an interesting question which requires you to give a surface level answer to a much deeper question like someone asking you why you are taking a certain class, majoring in a certain field or working a particular job; the answer goes deeper than just, "Oh, because I thought it would be good for my future."

As the question made its way around the 65 participants, I did what I normally do in this situation, think about what

I am going to say usually unable to pay attention to what other people are saying. But one thing did grab my attention. Even lost in a mix of thoughts and nerves about introducing myself to the group I did manage to hear one of my fellow participants say the following:

"I think that we have become human doings, rather than human beings and I am here to try to be more like the latter."

Umm wow... somebody quote this man, oh wait I just did...

This quote made me think. A lot of us spend our lives feeling like we need to do something, like our calendars always need to be full. And when we end up with free time, we struggle to find meaning in it, often looking for something to do rather than just being.

So that is the purpose of this section. It is an attempt to be a human being, a practice of just being rather than trying to desperately find something to do. Now, there is nothing wrong with doing things and being a very productive human being. And there is definitely nothing wrong with having your Google calendar filled to the brim with appointments, meetings and meals with friends. Think back to how busy the Dalai Lama is.

The problem arises when we finally get to a lapse in our schedule, to a place where we no longer have a next thing to get to, or something else to occupy our mind. It is in this lull that we need to learn how to be human beings, not human doings.

How to be a Human BEING:

- Next time that you get to an open space in your calendar, a moment of free time in your busy life, try and do nothing. Do not immediately check your phone for updates or send texts to friends to hang out, but rather take a few moments to just be present in the world around you.
- Some of the best times to try this exercise are on public transportation or waiting at a doctor's office, times when we are alone with nothing to do but are forced to be where we are. These are the times when we would often default to our phone but instead just try being there.
- See how this feels, see what it feels like to not need to just do things, but rather see what it feels like just to be present in the world, experiencing everything going on internally and externally.

I do not expect this to be an easy exercise and frankly, there are times when my schedule frees up and I feel the need to go on to the next activity immediately.

So start small.

Start with a small pause during these moments, just a few seconds in between activities to familiarize yourself with what it means to just be. As you do this, you will start to get more comfortable with this practice, allowing you to remain present for longer and longer feeling content with just being rather than craving for things to do. Look around, look inside, and see how it feels to be alive in this moment right now.

Why is this important?

Maya Angelou once said, "People will forget what you say, they will forget what you do, but they will never forget how you make them feel." The more that you observe yourself, the more that you act like a human being and not a human doing, the more that you will be able to impact the world around you! When you stop trying to do the next thing, you can stop for a minute and truly see how you are feeling and when you are in touch with your own feelings, you can help others with theirs.

Paulo Coelho, the author of the bestselling book *The Alchemist*, has another incredible novel called *The Pilgrimage*, a story that depicts Paulo's journey across Spain along the Road of San Tiago.

In the book, there is a dialogue between Paulo and his guide in which the guide looks up into the night sky and recounts how "every star — and every person — has their own space and their own special characteristics… What appears from down here to be a huge number of bodies that are similar to each other are really a million different things, spread over a space that is beyond human comprehension."

Often times, we try to differentiate ourselves by the things that we do, but as the dialogue continues, Paulo's guide proposes another idea. Expanding on his analogy about the stars in the night sky, the guide says, "…earlier; we only heard their noise because of the day light. Now we can see their light. That's the only change people can aspire to."

Going back to the quote by Maya Angelou, people will forget what you say and what you do, they will forget the noise that you make, and they will forget your actions. But they will never forget the light that you cast, the feelings that you provide. That is what this exercise is building up to, it is a practice of trying to be a light, trying just to be in the world, not feeling the need to always do something or say something. Rather, by just being, being a light that people can see, we can have an even greater impact on those around us.

# PART III

## THE ROLE MEDITATORS

*"The goal is not to be better than the other man, but your previous self."*

— HIS HOLINESS THE DALAI LAMA

CHAPTER 9

# FINDING FLOW, MEDITATION IN SPORTS

---

*"George helped me understand the art of mindfulness. To be neither distracted or focused, rigid or flexible, passive or aggressive. I learned just to be."*

— KOBE BRYANT, 5-TIME NBA CHAMPION,

LOS ANGELES LAKERS

George Mumford is credited in some circles as a key contributor on at least eight NBA championships.

The funny thing is, Mumford never played basketball beyond college.

Mumford played basketball at the University of Massachusetts. Ironically, he was roommates with Julius Erving (also known as Hall-of-Famer, Dr. J.). Mumford was injured and unable to continue to play while in college. The constant pain from his injury so severe that he was on daily medication that he says numbed him to the point of emptiness, and eventually led to his heroin addiction.

After getting clean, Mumford would enroll in Dr. Jon Kabat-Zinn's Mindfulness Based Stress Reduction program where he'd begin to study the power of the mind, to control pain and create focus. Kabat-Zinn would become a mentor, and the two would collaborate to create the Inner-city Stress Reduction Clinic.

It was a 1993 phone call that would change Mumford's future — and that of several future NBA Hall of Fame players.

Coach Phil Jackson was a well-known user of mindfulness techniques, giving his players the book *Zen and the Art of Motorcycle Maintenance* to understand some of the principles that had made Jackson the league's top coach. However, in 1993 his Chicago Bulls were struggling after having lost Michael Jordan to baseball following the death of Jordan's father. After this shocking announcement, Coach Jackson reached out to Dr. Kabat-Zinn to find someone who could teach mindfulness techniques to his team — asking for someone who not only understood meditation and mindfulness but could also communicate in the language of his players.

Kabat-Zinn connected Jackson to Mumford and their partnership began.

Mumford went on to help the Chicago Bulls win three straight championships, before joining the Los Angeles Lakers who would win five more.

**

Sports have long used verbiage consistent with meditation and mindfulness.

"He was in the zone..."

"She was locked in..."

"They were dialed in..."

"The team tuned out all distractions..."

Meditation has flourished in the sports community, becoming a tool to help athletes harness both the power of their bodies and the power of their minds. At the professional level, athletes have honed their skills to the point of near perfection, with thousands of hours of practice and a dedication to keeping their body in peak physical shape. While every player in the NBA is much better at basketball than the average person, there is still a spectrum of how good a player can be. Not every player is Michael Jordan and not every team is the current Golden State Warriors. A big component of that difference is having a strong mental ability, the ability to be totally in the zone, ready to perform when it is most important.

If you are an athlete, the sensations you have felt on the field or the court can be recreated and honed using meditation.

Meditation has been an integral part of training for high performing athletes for quite some time. Though sometimes it is not called meditation, the same principles are still being applied when an athlete is trying to play in the moment. George Mumford understood this and was able to use his own experiences and his training to connect with players like Michael Jordan and Kobe Bryant.

George Mumford talks openly about his early 20's and being a "functioning heroin addict" meaning that he was able to function in his day to day roles while high. He was able to continue working a high-paying job on Wall Street helping to both fuel and pay for his addiction. Even after a long struggle to get clean, George was still dealing with the chronic pain from his college days. However, this time, his pain did not lead him to drugs, instead, it led him to a mindfulness class where they talked about the importance of the mind-body connection. Here George realized the capacity he had over his own being; he realized that often a lot of his pain – for instance, chronic migraines – could be prevented not through medication but by utilizing the power of his mind through meditation to control his body.

Afterward, Mumford spent his time trying to learn every-thing he could about meditation and the mind. As he puts "I'm a perfectionist, I never do anything halfway." He spent some time living in meditation communities, practicing, reading, teaching and honing the skills of which he had just begun to scratch the surface. He even sat a few three-month long retreats, diving headfirst into this newfound practice.

A few years later, George found himself working to teach meditation to prisoners and at-risk students, using his back-ground and upbringing to try to connect to them on a deeper level, showing them the practical application of this tool. As you now know, it was during this period in his life that he met Phil Jackson, and as they say, the rest is history.

**

Often Mumford hears the question "How do you get professional athletes to sit on the floor and meditate?"

With such elegance, Mumford details that he is not teaching them anything that they do not already know. He is simply showing them a way to look at what is already there. All athletes can understand being in the zone. They can comprehend what it means to play in the present moment. With a little coaching, they can see that meditation is not just for monks.

"Whatever is on your mind, that is your meditation," Mumford says. He goes on to quote Dr. Dre & Snoop Dogg saying, "I got my mind on money and money on my mind."

According to Mumford, Dre & Snoop in their song "Gin and Juice" understand the concept of meditation. For them, the object of meditation would be money and the continuous focus, dedication, and visualization of the object can help bring you closer to it.

In reality, money might not be the best object of focus because money does not create lasting happiness, but the point is that whatever your intention, that is where you give your attention. The problem arises when your intention and your attention are not aligned.

In basketball, if your intention is to make this free throw, but your attention is focused on winning the game, you are going to have a much harder time sinking the shot. It is with this analogy that Mumford can bring forward this idea of "flow," or "being totally in the present moment allowing you to act from a place of ingrained feeling rather than intellectualized thought."

Sound familiar to our definition of meditation from the beginning? Using language like this, Mumford is able to convince many professional athletes to sit in a dark room and focus on their breathing.

After having practiced the mechanics for so long, the only thing that could get in an athlete's way is his or her own mind. Therefore, this practice allows one to get out of his or her head and just focus on playing, right here, right now in the moment.

It is much harder to teach an athlete how to be in flow, just as it would be hard to tell an aspiring meditator to just 'be present'; instead you need to learn practices that can prepare you for the present moment. Mumford refers to this as being 'flow ready', or creating the conditions for flow. Just as an athlete would practice relevant drills and train their physique to get ready for a game, they need to prepare their mind, in the same way, being "flow ready."

## MICHAEL JORDAN AND THE '90S BULLS

Mumford taught meditation to the greats. This long list includes the man who is known even to those who do not know a single thing about basketball: Michael Jordan. Everyone knows Michael Jordan, everyone has heard of his greatness but not a lot of people are aware of the intense mental training that goes into being at this level of competition.

Mumford joined Phil Jackson and the Bulls in 1993 during a dramatic time for the team. Having just lot Michael Jordan to baseball, the team was going to struggle in the upcoming season. The partnership between Mumford and Coach Jackson helped and the 1994 Bulls once again made it to the playoffs but without Jordan, they lost to the Knicks in the second round.

Michael Jordan returned to basketball midway through the 1995 season. Reuniting with the Bulls, Jordan joined the same training that all of the other players had gone through. They were all learning techniques like breath awareness meditations and visualization practices in order to become mentally prepared for game time, in order to be "flow ready."

\*\*

When Michael Jordan first announced his retirement in the aftermath of the 1992–93 season, he said that he "lost his love for the game." Jordan had been considering retirement for quite some time and the death of his father further solidified this desire. As Jordan started to deal with all of these emotions and changes, he decided that his best bet was to hang up his jersey and move on to something else.

Michael Jordan joined Major League Baseball in 1994, signing a deal with the Chicago White Sox. Jordan was trying to honor the dreams of his late father, who had always envisioned his son as a Major League Baseball player.

Unfortunately, the change of sports wasn't going to fix the hole that had been left in Jordan's heart. He had lost his father, he had lost a game that he loved, and he had lost himself. Luckily, he didn't have to go anywhere but inside in order to find it.

Graham Betchart, author of *Play Present, A Mental Skills Training Program for Basketball Players* had the pleasure of meeting Michael Jordan some years after he retired from the sport.

Feeling a much larger hand engulf his, Graham found himself staring into the eyes of one of his idols, a man who made basketball what it is today. Graham explained what he does for a living, telling Jordan that he works to bring mindfulness and meditation practices to athletes. Graham even cited that he worked with Jordan's once mindfulness coach, George Mumford. Jordan brought Graham in close and spoke into his ear so only Graham could hear, "George Mumford and what he does, saved my life."

**

Playing off the ideas of Mihaly Csikszentmihalyi — a Hungarian-American Psychologist and the man to recognize and name the psychological concept of flow — Mumford explains how we spend most of our life out of flow, in states of boredom and anxiety.

Boredom occurs when your skills exceed the situation and the stakes are low. Think about working a job below your skill-set with no real future prospects, it can often feel very boring. Or think about a professional basketball team playing an exhibition against a handful of high-schoolers.

Anxiety occurs when the stakes are high and your skill set is not up to par. Think about being thrown into open-heart surgery without having any doctoral schooling or experience. Or being those high schoolers who are playing professionals while college scouts are watching.

While these examples are very drastic, it paints the overall picture that in these states, it is hard to perform. Either it doesn't feel like enough of a challenge and you stop trying or it is so hard that you just give up, but in the middle of these states is the beautiful flow that Mumford explained earlier. The state where you are completely present in the midst of chaos.

This is what Mumford taught the Bulls.

**

With Jordan back on the team, the Bulls went on to achieve another three-peat winning the championship in '96, '97, and '98.

It would be a stretch to say that George Mumford had any hand in creating the greatness that encompassed Michael Jordan and this Bulls' team. However, Mumford did something incredible. He showed the players the capacity of their own minds.

Michael Jordan just like any one of us goes through emotional turmoil. He too faces life's rollercoaster with all its ups and downs. The only difference is that on most nights he had to step out in front of a giant crowd to play a game in front of a televised audience. So much was expected of him that even the slightest chink in his mental armor could be detrimental. One distracting thought, one moment out of the present could mean the difference between winning and losing the championship.

I like to think of Mumford, and on a larger scale meditation, as a blacksmith, helping to fully build and repair the mental armor of these individuals. Like the amazing sculptor and artist, Michelangelo, Mumford does not create greatness, he just chips away to reveal the masterpiece within. The capacity for flow was already there – Mumford just showed the players how to access it.

## KOBE BRYANT

When Phil Jackson left the windy city for LA, Mumford went with him, becoming the mindfulness consultant for the Los Angeles Lakers. During this time, Mumford was able to work with another one of the best basketball players this world has ever seen: Kobe Bryant.

Kobe is extremely vocal about meditation and how much meditation has impacted his life. On Oprah's show, he revealed that he meditates every single morning for 10–15 minutes.

As Bryant puts it, "if I don't do it [meditation], I feel like I'm constantly chasing the day. As opposed to being able to control and dictate the day. Not that you're calling the shots on what comes forward... but the fact that I am set and ready for whatever may come my way."

Here is a star NBA player, arguably one of the top 5 players in the history of the game, proclaiming the importance of this practice and the impact that it has had on him.

For a minute, imagine you are a professional sports player (if you already are a player, just think about your own life). Picture the stress and chaos that is a professional sports game.

You have thousands of fans in the stadium cheering you on and if it's an away game, thousands more booing you. There are even more people watching you at home on TV. You have your family, friends, teammates there who are all looking to you to play at your best. You have all of this pressure that it can often feel like you are caught in the midst of a hurricane.

Flow doesn't take you away from the hurricane, no, it places you right in the middle of it, right smack in the eye. But, amidst all of the destruction and power of a hurricane, the middle of the storm, the heart of it is completely calm. It is a little sliver of pure calmness among all the chaos.

This is the state of mind that Mumford wanted his players to achieve. This is the state of mind that Kobe was able to achieve. So that even with the game on the line and thousands of people relying on you, you could feel no pressure at all, trusting your skills and allowing yourself to play in the moment.

**

If you are a visual learner, then I recommend you watch Kobe Bryant's final career game.

Down 12 points and only three minutes left, Kobe takes control, leading his team to victory, scoring 14 points in a row and sinking the game-winning shot, to lock in 60 points for the game. As you watch the recap, you can see how calm he is. Kobe knows that this is his last game, that his team is down and that the chances of winning are slim, but he does not let this get in his way. Instead, he posts one of the best performances of his career with ease, totally trusting his skills and just playing in the moment.

You can see it in his face. A calmness as abnormal as the eye of a hurricane, a place where you would expect the most chaos but instead you see a respite from the storm. It is Kobe's last game of his career. This thought alone is enough to derail a person, take them out of flow, and put them straight into a state of anxiety.

But not Kobe.

He is totally locked in, totally focused, 100% in flow.

1 shot at a time, 1 step at a time, 1 second at a time.

## YOU DON'T HAVE TO BE A HALL-OF-FAMER

You by no means have to be an athlete to connect to the material in this chapter. In reality, even if you aren't a sports fan, there is something in here for you. While the language and implementation might be different, we are all drinking from the same hose, we all are striving for the same thing, happiness in the present moment.

At the end of the day, we are all competitors in life, we all work our butts off and show up ready to perform whether it be in an Econ 101 lecture, a spin class or a professional sports game. We can all benefit from being "flow ready", being ready to 'play' in whatever life throws our way.

CHAPTER 10

# FINDING VALUE, MEDITATION IN BUSINESS

———

*"I am working to put a man on the moon."*

— A JANITOR AT NASA DURING JFK'S PRESIDENCY

We are a society that always strives for more.

We want to keep going up and up, uncomfortable with staying stagnant.

There is nothing wrong with this idea on the surface because it can propel us to new heights and push us forward. However, this mindset is what puts us on autopilot, blindly striving for our goals, ignoring important lessons and insights that might pop up along the way.

There are many examples of individuals who put in years of long hours and hard work to be gifted with promotions or maybe even the leading role of a company. For many people, this is a goal they have had from a young age and this success would be something to celebrate. However, often it is difficult to get out of the mindset of continuing to go forward and it can even feel nothing will ever be enough. Even when you are the CEO of a high-profile company, you might feel the need to go onto the next thing: maybe the need to switch companies, always striving to do something new and different, totally oblivious to just being in the moment. It takes me back to the story of Jim from Chapter One. What else have we missed during our journey? What did we ignore at the time in order to get to somewhere else?

**

Nelson Mandela said, "It seems impossible until it is done."

Often walking into a company as an analyst, it can feel like a long and near impossible road to CEO. However, as Mandela says it only seems impossible, and then one day you find yourself sitting in the comfy chair in the big corner office. That said, what did you miss in order to get there?

If you have ever seen the movie *Click* with Adam Sandler, you will remember that his character can control his life using a little remote that he got from the Beyond section of Bed Bath & Beyond. He decides to fast-forward through a portion of his career until he receives the promotion he had long sought after. Clicking the two double arrows on the remote, time speeds up, until he finds himself at his promotion party a full year later. He continues to speed up his entire life until he reaches his death. In a tear-provoking scene, Adam Sandler's character shows a deep regret for not enjoying the moment, for trying to just fast-forward to the "good parts."

This is an over-dramatized example using a fictional Hollywood movie, but there is a lot of truth in the message. One day we could be sitting in the CEO office, looking back, asking, "Where did all the time go?" Maybe you feel that way right now, whether it be looking back on your career, or your time in college, or your younger life. We can easily sympathize with this question, "Where did the time go?"

Time is an arrow that marches forward, never back, that is why it is important to embrace the present moment even when our goals are far in the future. When you live life out of the present moment, spending all your time reminiscing about the past and planning for the future, it can be easy to let these moments pass us by, to let life pass us by.

This is why meditation is crucial not just at the executive level, but also at the analyst or even the intern level. Being able to embrace your role and truly give your all to the present moment will have a huge impact on your career.

You might be thinking that you can be a good employee without living in the present; you can work your ass off and get promotions without having to meditate every day. The difference comes in the ability to enjoy where you are. Often we can put on a fake smile and just go through the motions of work and life, saying we enjoy where we are, but this is a facade for wanting desperately to be somewhere else. What if instead, we could embrace the present, seeing this moment not as just a stepping-stone, but rather a respite from the constant running. A moment to stay and learn, trying to see where this road can take us instead of just wanting to be at the end of it.

**

I have been dealing with a lot of this myself. Having just started my first job out of college, I have been struggling to truly enjoy the long hours of Excel spreadsheets. It has been a difficult thing to be at the bottom of the totem pole, to be a new employee who just needs to follow orders respectfully. This seems to be a trend in our world. We start at the bottom being the youngest kids in school. Slowly over the years, you rise to the top whether 5th grade, 8th grade, 12th grade, or college seniors, you slowly transition from the bottom of the totem pole to the top. Once you are at the top, your experience is short-lived; you get a year and then you move on to the next thing, you move from middle school to high school or from college to the workforce and it feels like you start all over again. It is like the minute you are finally comfortable and confident with where you are, you have to change.

I am not going to say that I have found a solution to this "problem." Though it doesn't have to suck. We do not have to hate where we are at this moment. As the days have gone by, I have taught myself to enjoy the mechanics of Excel spreadsheets, striving to make my spreadsheets the best that I can, trying to go above and beyond rather than just doing monotonous work. I have also tried to appreciate my position even though it does not hold the title of executive. Yes, I am a first-year analyst, but it is in this position where I will learn, where I can sit and observe without pressure to speak on behalf of the company.

Life is all about how you look at it. While I still have tough days at work, days where all I want to do is go home to curl up in bed and sleep forever, I have continued to stick with it, getting up every morning and walking in with a smile on my face. Often times we cannot change our roles. We cannot change companies and risk unemployment, so the only thing left is to change your attitude. If you learn to be happy with where you are, then you will be overjoyed when you finally get to where you want to be.

## JFK'S JANITOR

We all have a role to play, not just in our own lives, but also in the lives of those around us. This role, just like us, is always changing and it is important to notice exactly where we are in this moment.

I recently spent some time helping at my parents' newly opened restaurant, Lo-Cal Kitchen, doing everything from interacting with customers as a manager to washing dishes down in the kitchen. It was easy for me to enjoy my roles seeing as I felt my contribution to the overall mission my family was striving for: "to bring healthy, yet tasty options to the world." However, some of the employees were struggling to find meaning in their jobs. This sentiment isn't without reason though. How can a 19-year-old kid, who isn't going to college find joy and meaning in washing dishes? How can he or she enjoy where they are at that moment without worrying about the future?

This dilemma isn't unique to my parent's restaurant. Financial service firms, like Goldman Sachs, JP Morgan and others are big attractions for first-year-out-of-college individuals, but the firms struggle with retention. In fact, most analysts are already looking for their second job within the first few months of starting the first one.

I hear older generations complain about how no kid works a job for more than a few years, how everyone is bouncing from place to place, when "back in the day" it was normal to remain at the same company for many years, maybe even your whole career. Now, however, we are constantly looking for the next thing, the next role that is going to help us on our journey to some unclear destination. How then can we possibly enjoy where we are right now in this very moment? Instead of being a means to an end, why can't every role be the end goal for right now, working hard, truly enjoying the job, eager to see where it takes you?

There is a story about a janitor who worked for NASA during John F. Kennedy's presidency. While on a tour of the NASA facility, JFK noticed the janitor who had a huge smile on his face. This man seemed to take complete pride in his work, truly enjoying his job.

"What do you think you are doing here?" JFK asked, referring to the janitor's obligations in this role.

"I am working to put a man on the moon," the janitor replied.

Here was a man who was cleaning floors and scrubbing toilets for a living and yet he took pride in his work. He knew that he was part of some greater mission; some bigger idea and this gave him purpose. When we can find meaning in what we are doing in this exact moment, the job starts to have a purpose; life starts to have a purpose. There becomes a drive, a desire to get out of bed every morning and go to work.

Tony Hsieh, CEO of the online clothing and shoe store Zappos, describes three types of happiness or fulfillment: pleasure, passion, and higher purpose.

1. Pleasure is the elated temporary feeling you get when you think about eating that piece of cake or buying a new outfit.
2. Passion is when you are doing something you enjoy and the time flies by, like reading a good book or working on a fulfilling project.
3. Higher purpose is the feeling of being part of something bigger than you are. This is why this janitor and me enjoyed jobs like mopping floors and washing dishes that on the surface would not seem enjoyable.

All of these forms of happiness are worth striving for, but the most long lasting and fulfilling form is higher purpose.

When you can comprehend your value and meaning in this world, you start to feel how important you are to the people around you, to the company that you are working for, to yourself. When you are part of some higher purpose, you truly start to feel complete, you start to enjoy what you do and you truly take pride in your work no matter how big or little the role is.

This is where meditation comes in.

Practices of meditation can and have been applied in the workplace. Meditation does not need to be a separate part of your life, but rather it can help you both personally and professionally, allowing you to see a higher purpose in work and in life.

## JANICE MARTURANO

*"Meditation provides the space for all of us to be better leaders."*

— JANICE MARTURANO

This is the motto of Janice Marturano's Institute for Mindful Leadership, an organization that she created after leaving General Mills – you know General Mills, the company that makes practically every single cereal we used to eat as kids.

Janice Marturano describes herself as a 21st-century juggler.

She had been recently promoted to Vice President at General Mills. She was the president of a nonprofit. She was married, had two school-aged kids and was the daughter of aging parents. She felt like she was doing everything that she was supposed to, checking all of the boxes, yet it felt like she couldn't control anything. She was juggling so many different roles and responsibilities that it was hard to fulfill them all. I think quite a few of us can relate.

Janice describes a time in her life when she remembers being particularly stressed. Early one morning, she received a phone call regarding the potential for General Mills to acquire Pillsbury. She didn't know it then but at that moment she was about to go through an 18-month journey to try and close this deal. A deal that could cost 10,000 people their jobs. And a journey that would definitely change her life.

It was during this time that Janice was faced with the loss of both her mother and father. She describes this feeling of being unable to even grieve, unable to give time to her role as a daughter. Instead, she needed to stay focused on getting this deal done, figuring that afterward she would have some time to cope with all of this and bounce back.

The deal which should've closed in 6 months lasted 18. Even when the deal went through and all of her hard work paid off, Janice went straight back to the act of "juggling." While she was still managing to handle all of her responsibilities, she describes a feeling of great depletion as if she could no longer easily bounce back from difficult situations and long work days.

We can all sympathize with the feeling of being overwhelmed, shutting down, unable to find the drive to fulfill our requirements. This feeling can drag on for months and for Janice, it did.

She finally decided to see a doctor, hoping medicine had a cure. The doctor recommended that she go to a spa and try to relax, shutting out some of the constant stimuli that had caused the depletion in the first place. To Janice, this was a crazy idea, she needed help managing her responsibilities. She couldn't take a vacation. How could she possibly leave all of this for a spa break?

So she decided against taking some time off, figuring she could push through the struggles. Later that week she happened to see an advertisement for a mindfulness course aimed at educating executives. She figured this course would allow her to take that recommended and much-needed break, while still learning something productive along the way.

Little did she know she was about to learn practices of meditation and mindfulness; practices that would change her entire life.

She returned to her routine with this new secret weapon, meditation.

**

In the workplace though?

Could this practice really help in a corporate setting?

Janice recounts a story of working with a very difficult individual. I am sure we have all been in this position, whether at work or in school; a time when a group or team member was extremely difficult to work with and it had a huge impact on our own mental state.

Janice said that it was so bad that even seeing the name of this person on a meeting invite would give her chest pains.

She recounts walking to the meeting unable to think of anything but the bad experiences that she and this co-worker have had. It was so overpowering that when she arrived at the door, she felt nothing but tightness, like a catapult being pulled back waiting to launch forward. Obviously, Janice wasn't going to leap at her co-worker, but there was no way that a meeting could be productive with feelings like these. Time after time, the emotion would overpower the ability to work together, getting in the way of compromise and productivity.

What if there was a different way? A way that was easier and actually took much less effort.

For Janice, the answer was loving-kindness practice. As we have discussed earlier, this is a practice that allows us to cultivate love and kindness for ourselves and others on this planet. Janice employed this practice prior to her next meeting with this individual. Instead of walking toward the conference room stewing over past interactions, she would think to herself, "may my co-worker be happy, may she find whatever her heart desires" wishing well for her co-worker, wishing thoughts of love and kindness that Janice would want wished on herself.

Nothing was different about the meeting or its participants, but when Janice locked eyes with her "enemy," she didn't feel the same uneasy feelings. The meeting was productive, Janice didn't feel so tight and she actually left feeling good about the interaction. Janice did not change the meeting structure, she didn't try to make jokes or bridge the tension; she simply changed the way in which she arrived to the meeting. She showed up with a little more openness and a whole lot of love.

I am sure you may still be asking, "How is this easier?" You may believe that it takes so much effort to be kind especially to those with whom we struggle. Well next time something like this happens, think about how heavy you feel after a negative interaction, how taxing it can be. Then remember that you cannot change anyone but yourself and the only way to alter this interaction and make it not as burdensome is for **you** simply to change how **you** approach it. And since we know that negativity takes a huge toll on us, why not try the exact opposite and you will see that it truly is so much easier. You feel lighter and freer, and you actually leave feeling so much better.

Fun fact: It takes 17 muscles to frown and only 13 to smile.

Meditation can be truly impactful in the world of business. It can help us to be better leaders and employees. Corporations are simply groups of individuals, individuals who are often reactive and not responsive. Meditation teaches us how to be more responsive it helps us to deal with disputes with co-workers, company-wide decisions, personal choices and so much more. We spend much of our lives at work, so it is crucial to find things that will help better our experience and as Janice's story portrays, meditation definitely fits that description.

## RAY DALIO

*"Meditation more than anything in my life was the biggest ingredient of whatever success I've had."*

— RAY DALIO

Ray Dalio is the Founder and Chief Investment Officer of Bridgewater Associates, an investment management firm that boasts over $150 Billion in assets under management and manages over 350 of the world's top clients.

\*\*

For those who don't know what that means, don't worry: I didn't either. Basically, Bridgewater invests money on behalf of many sophisticated global institutional clients like pension funds and university endowments. Bridgewater prides itself on being experts in the market and understanding the global economy. They use this knowledge to drive returns, or profits, for their investors.

\*\*

Ray Dalio founded the company in 1975 after working on the New York Stock Exchange. He launched the company out of an extra bedroom in his Manhattan apartment. In 2005, Ray's company became recognized as the largest hedge fund in the world and still boasts that title to this day.

How did Ray manage to do this? How did he manage to build a company out of nothing, in a spare bedroom in his apartment and turn it into the largest investment fund in the entire world?

Well, I am not going to tell you that meditation was the answer, because Mr. Dalio already told you that himself. Ray attributes his success – his ability to turn nothing into something, his ability to build a thriving company – to meditation. Even if at this moment, we are not inclined to go out and start a company that will grow to be the biggest hedge fund in the world, every one of us can agree that achieving this feat would be incredible.

Dalio has publicly discussed how meditation has affected his life and career. In an interview with the John Main Center of Meditation at Georgetown University, Ray says that "meditation gives him centeredness." It allows him to look at things throughout the day without the being hijacked by his emotions. It allows him to engage in difficult decisions and conversations with an art of clarity and calmness that comes from that centered place.

This practice allows Ray Dalio to be a better CEO, a better family member, and a better person. It allows him to create some space between the situations he encounters and his reaction, distance between stimulus and response.

Ray Dalio and Bridgewater Associates were prepared for the most recent financial crisis in 2008. Unlike most of their peers, Bridgewater did not jump at the opportunity to make money off risky investments or in products that were unfamiliar. This caused the company to steer away from buying credit default swaps and other levered investment instruments. Instead, Bridgewater had been doing research, compiling data about the rising debt markets, and referring back to recent financial dips to see if there was a trend. Dalio even talks about his own diligence and how he took the time to go through newspaper articles from the days leading up to the Great Depression and history books detailing the financial struggles of the Weimar Republic in Germany, trying to find parallels to the 2008 economic environment.

By the fall of Lehman Brothers on September 15, 2008, Dalio and Bridgewater had already been talking about a financial down turn for months. As a former senior employee under the U.S. Secretary of Treasury (2007–2009) and Co-CEO of Bridgewater, David McCormick put it, "The thing that Bridgewater has is this constant search for understanding." Instead of just focusing on blindly increasing profits, Bridgewater wanted to see where the money was coming from. How could the environment leading up to the financial crash be producing so much capital for financial service firms? It is this desire to understand, the ability to take a step back and look before acting that allowed Bridgewater to remain standing during the recession.

This mindset of understanding and seeing the bigger picture is also something that we can learn through meditation, as it teaches us to spend time and look at what is happening in the present moment. This is something that Ray Dalio learned through his practice and qualities that the company embodies. Dalio has offered meditation to his entire office but does not require it. It is a gift that he wants to share with everyone but force on no one. It has helped him in business and in his personal endeavors and I am sure it can help you too.

## CHADE-MENG TAN

*Employee #107*

Google's Jolly Good Fellow has the goal of creating world peace in his lifetime. Chade-Meng Tan was employee number 107 at Google. He was one of the first software engineers to join the Google team in 2000. However, after eight years working in this role helping to develop platforms such as mobile search, Meng was "promoted" to the title on his business card: "Jolly Good Fellow."

This eccentric title was given to him after he started a mindfulness-training course that was taught to all of Google's employees. Meng's new role consisted of giving employees the tools to feel like empowered and responsible individuals who want to contribute to the good of the company. Meng was also the first point of contact for outsiders to the company. The warm smile and demeanor of Google's Jolly Good Fellow would meet anyone coming to speak to Google. This role resulted in Meng's collection of photos with famous people like President Carter, the Dalai Lama, Al Gore and many more.

So what is Meng's secret, how does a software engineer wake up one morning and decide that instead of designing mobile search he would rather greet famous people and develop a mindfulness course?

Meng became interested in mindfulness after reading about people like Matthieu Ricard, our resident happiest man in the world. Like me, Meng was interested in how simply sitting and thinking about compassion can make one the happiest person in the world. This provides the scary yet reassuring thought that we do not need to go beyond our own minds to find what we are all searching for, rather we can "search inside ourselves."

And thus, *Search Inside Yourself* was born. *Search Inside Yourself* started as a Google-specific course and is now a book that shows the usefulness of meditation, mindfulness, emotional intelligence and other tools in the workplace. It has many excellent practices that can help one remain mindful in the hectic, fast-paced world of the 21st century.

Meng brought groundbreaking practices to the Google team, convincing them to expand their cognitive and emotional abilities. He educated them on how to create a quality of mind that is both calm and clear, he showed them many meditation techniques and his personal favorite, and he showed them how compassion can be fun.

According to Meng, when compassion is fun, world peace can be achieved.

World peace is Meng's ultimate goal. Obviously, he thought this sounded crazy when he first said it aloud. The thought that he could create world peace in his lifetime was absurd. However, the more he taught, the more he worked to spread compassion, the more real this idea became.

Meng's course has an element that requires its participants to create new mental habits. He gives the example of meeting someone new and trying to think, "I want you to be happy." We all have a person we struggle with, whether it be the coworker in Janice Marturano's story or even just a random stranger who wrongs us. Meng says that by wishing this individual compassion we can learn to find a place for this person in our hearts, even if it is just a small one. This small activity can actually change your demeanor to the world around you. If you walk around silently wishing happiness on everyone, it will be completely visible through your smile, your posture, and the way you present yourself. We all know the warm feelings we get when someone does something kind for us or simply smiles at us on the street. Well, by being this person to other people, you slowly start to create the conditions for kindness. Think about yourself as the first domino in a row of 7 billion. By being kind, you spread the conditions of kindness to others who spread it to others until eventually the world is overpowered by kindness, by peace, world peace.

**

At age 45, Meng retired from his role at Google. Taking down his photographs and emptying the draws of his business cards, in hopes of starting his own company.

Meng is the founder of the Search Inside Yourself Leadership Institute, an organization he started to spread his ideas beyond the doors of Google headquarters. Meng still works to achieve his goal of world peace and we can all be part of that.

## STEVE JOBS

*"If you just sit and observe, you will see how restless your mind is. If you try to calm it, it only makes it worse, but over time it does calm, and when it does, there's room to hear more subtle things – that's when your intuition starts to blossom and you start to see things more clearly and be in the present more. Your mind just slows down, and you see a tremendous expanse in the moment. You see so much more than you could see before. It's a discipline; you have to practice it."*

— STEVE JOBS

In 1974, Steve Jobs returned to California. Jobs was almost unrecognizable to his parents, Clara and Paul, as he stepped off the plane in San Francisco. Jobs had dropped out of Reed College and decided to spend a few months in India. This was long before his founding of Apple, long before the world knew him. Back then, Steve Jobs was not the face of one of the world's most successful companies. Instead, he was a young kid, a college dropout, and a student of meditation.

During the 1970s, Zen Buddhism began to flourish in San Francisco as practitioners started to bring the teachings over from the Eastern world. The United States started to become exposed to these ancient tools and techniques. Jobs was hooked.

In the final years of his life, Steve Jobs explained to Walter Isaacson, the man who wrote Jobs' biography, that he would meditate regularly. Jobs found it to be an extremely powerful and useful discipline, one that stuck with him from the '70s until his death in 2011.

When Jobs returned home from his travels to India, he wanted to continue cultivating this meditation practice. He met with Shunryu Suzuki, a famed Soto Zen monk well known for the popularization of Zen Buddhism in the United States. Soto Zen or the Soto school is one of the original sects of Zen Buddhism. It differentiates itself from the pack by being a practice of meditation that has no object, anchor, or content. Rather, the meditator strives to be aware of his stream of thoughts; simply letting them arise and pass. Job's was fortunate enough to receive the teaching of one of Soto Zen master Suzuki's students, Kobun Otogawa. Jobs met with Otogawa almost every day and every few months, they would go on a meditation retreat together, a time spent just meditating and being present.

At one point, Steve Jobs considered moving to Japan. He had such an affinity to Zen that he wanted to become a monk and focus just on his practice. When he brought this idea to his close friend and teacher, Otogawa, he persuaded Jobs against it. Otogawa believed that Steve Jobs had important work to do in California and becoming a Zen monk was not the path for him, not in this life. Turns out Kobun Otogawa is a pretty insightful guy.

Though Jobs did not become a monk, he did continue to let the practice influence every part of his life. Zen Buddhism stresses the importance of simplicity, courage, resoluteness, and austerity, teaching practitioners to embody these qualities in every aspect of their lives. Practitioners should be in the moment and be mindful at all times, appreciating the world's beauty. It is believed that Apple's brand and products are based on these ideas. The simplicity of the logo, the curvature of all the products, the incredible detail in everything, they are all influenced by the essence of Zen. It would not be crazy to further assert that Jobs' Zen practice also helped him when he got fired from Apple in 1985 and allowed him to come back more than ten years later, retaking the helm with a new mindset, a new courage, a new desire to change the world.

There is no question that Steve Jobs is an innovator, an icon, a genius. He has an incredible story and meditation played a crucial role in the narrative. Meditation was a discipline that helped Jobs both personally and professionally. It was a guide for him throughout his journey.

## ACHIEVE YOUR POTENTIAL

In my role right now, I am achieving my potential. Not because I asked for a better job or more responsibility, but because I try to do my job as well as I can. Just because the role isn't your end goal, doesn't mean that it has no value. Even if your role requires you to wash dishes, be the best dishwasher this world has ever seen. Keep working your hardest, keep trying your best, someone will notice and somehow it will take you where you want to be.

Meditation has played a crucial role in the lives and success of the individuals in this chapter and so many more. Meditation is an anchor, a guide, a practice that they have all found useful and something that you too can benefit from. Meditation is not going to make you Steve Jobs or Ray Dalio, but it will make you, a better you. It will help you to unlock the best within yourself as it did for many of these individuals.

Whether you are the head of a company, an analyst or even a janitor, meditation can be useful for you.

# CHAPTER 11

# FINDING PROOF, MEDITATION AND SCIENCE

———

Many people approach meditation with skepticism. It is a practice that can create a lot of confusion and almost has this "used car salesperson" vibe to it. Here is this great thing someone is trying to sell you and yet the price seems too good to be true (free in the case of meditation).

It is a proposal that leads you to ask, "What's the catch?"

Meditation, unlike a used car, is not something you have to worry about. Meditation, unlike that car, is not something I am desperately trying to sell to you.

Meditation has been around for thousands of years and been practiced in many religions and cultures. Recently, however, scientists have tried to prove and confirm what practitioners have known all this time: this practice can truly have a positive impact.

If you are like me and think very logically and scientifically, it helps to hear about some of the research that is out there to support meditation and its effectiveness in our lives. Earlier in the century, the Dalai Lama made a huge push for scientists to start exploring this field of mindfulness and meditation. His Holiness found that when he would try to give people Buddhists texts, they would occasionally resist, but when he mentioned science, the conversation could begin. The Dalai Lama wants to spread meditation to the entire world, trying to include every individual on this planet by speaking in a language anyone can understand. This desire led to the birth of the Mind & Life Institute, an organization that works to merge meditation and the microscope. The idea is to combine the first-person experience of meditation with third-person objective scientific evidence. All of the research has come out in full support of meditation practices and the impacts and benefits it can have. There is even a field of study, contemplative neuroscience, dedicated just to this.

Often, we struggle to embrace things that we cannot logically understand. For a while now, meditation has fallen into this category. Meditation has been something that carries a stigma around it. Think back to my first few words, meditation has a branding problem. Many people associate meditation with this idea of crystals, robes, and people saying they can fly and see your future.

This is far from the truth.

Meditation is a field with a plethora of scientific backing and a long list of neuroscientists who are not only supporters but also practitioners.

If you are a skeptical person, do not worry. You can do meditation while being completely skeptical. You do not need to change who you are in order to access this practice, rather just come to it, with the attitude of a scientist: skeptical yet curious, and ready to find out the truth.

### DR. JON KABAT-ZINN

*"Mindfulness doesn't need to be promoted, it needs to be embodied."*

— JON KABAT-ZINN

Dr. Jon Kabat-Zinn may be considered one of the founding fathers of "Western Meditation." He was one of the first individuals to take techniques such as Buddhist meditation, and in a broader sense mindfulness, and place them in the context of a Western society.

Dr. Kabat-Zinn is the creator of Mindfulness-Based Stress Reduction (MBSR). This 8-week program uses techniques of meditation and mindfulness to help people overcome the difficulties and effects of stress.

It was first employed in a hospital setting in 1979, aimed at helping individuals cope with "untreatable" illnesses. In the '70s and '80s when Dr. Kabat-Zinn released this method, there were many cracks in the hospital system. The goal of a hospital was to treat you and if you were deemed untreatable then you were out of the purview of the system. This included patients who came in complaining about what we know as depression, anxiety disorders, or even chronic pain. These people were not getting the attention they needed, and something needed to be done.

This is where MBSR excelled. Dr. Kabat-Zinn took a group of these people, the ones whose ailments were considered beyond the scope of the hospital, and tried to help them with meditation techniques. The goal was not to cure people of their ailments, but rather to help them develop a greater understanding and acceptance of the diagnosis.

They found that the majority of participants experienced a reduction in the relevant psychological and medical symptoms of their respective medical diagnosis. Meaning that people with issues of chronic pain saw a notable reduction in pain levels and frequency, and patients with diagnoses of panic disorders or anxiety saw a decrease of these mental states. Not only was there a decrease in the medical symptoms, but also there was a notable increase in mental stability and a greater sense of coherence for these individuals. The latter implies that these individuals were able to find a greater sense of self and the ability to act calmly during situations of high stress.

They further saw that the 8-week long course had enough of an impact to last for several years, so even if you did not continue to practice, you would receive these residual benefits for up to four years. Imagine what you could do with a continued practice.

**

MBSR has definitely survived the trials of time, going on its 40th year of implementation. Since its inception, more than 24,000 people have completed this program.[15]

---

15  "History Of MBSR." 2018. *University Of Massachusetts Medical School.*

Why is this so effective? Why do people keep coming to get this training?

That goes back to the work of Elizabeth Blackburn, the Nobel Laureate, and Professor of Biology and Physiology at the University of California San Francisco who created a study to examine a huge problem with which we are all familiar:

**Stress takes years off our lives.**

To recap from Chapter Three: on the ends of our chromosomes, we have what are called telomeres. These telomeres are what allow our cells to divide which is necessary for growing new skin, blood, bone, and other cells. Without telomeres, the ends of the chromosomes could fuse together and corrupt the regeneration process, altering the body's genetic blueprint. When telomeres shorten (which they have been found to do rapidly in people with high-stress levels), it can lead to cell regeneration malfunction, which is a potential cause of cancer and aging.

Diving a little deeper, in our bodies we have an enzyme called Telomerase. This enzyme is responsible for adding bases to the ends of telomeres, helping to prevent them from degrading as our cells regenerate. Unfortunately, telomerase cannot keep up and as our cells continue to divide, not enough of the enzyme is present, this ultimately leads to the shortening of the telomeres and the aging of cells.

So if you think you are about to learn how to live forever, I am just going to shatter your hopes right now. Aging is simply part of life and while getting older and ultimately death is inevitable, there are ways that we can postpone this reality. Stress can play a huge role in the erosion of these telomeres this is called "stress-reducing longevity." In non-scientific terms, stress makes us age, and ultimately die faster, ergo "stress takes years off our lives."

Dr. Blackburn and her team set out to solve the following question: "Can meditation slow the rate of cellular aging?"

Yes.

We know that mindfulness meditation techniques can decrease ruminative thought (or being lost in thought) and increase awareness of the present moment. The scientists found that meditation, the practice of living in the present, can reduce stressful states and increase positive arousal states. This stress reduction can slow the erosion of our telomeres and ultimately slow down the process of aging.[16]

16 Blackburn Ph.D., Elizabeth, Elissa Epel Ph.D., Jennifer Daubenmier Ph.D., Judith T. Moskowitz Ph.D. and Susan Folkman Ph.D. "Can

∗∗

This is a grand assumption that I just made, but I would say that it has some weight to it. Meditation is a practice that has held its own in the trials of the scientific method.

Meditation has been around for thousands of years, not because scientists said that it works, but because the people doing it knew that it worked. Science is just supporting what many already know to be true, that meditation has a positive impact on our lives.

In this sense, Dr. Kabat-Zinn rightly put it, "Meditation doesn't need to be promoted, it needs to be embodied."

## DR. RICHARD DAVIDSON

Scientists used to think the brain stopped changing at age 20, that whoever you were at age 20 was who you were going to be for the rest of your life... Could you imagine? Imagine if you were stuck with the mind of a 20-year-old forever. Your 20s are the perfect time to make mistakes, to experiment, and to do stuff that the 40-year-old version of you would question thoroughly. It would be a travesty, to have a nation of people all thinking like 20 year olds.

meditation slow rate of cellular aging? Cognitive stress, mindfulness, and telomeres." *US National Library of Medicine.*

Dr. Richard Davidson is a Professor of Psychology and Psychiatry as well as the Founder and Director of the Center for Healthy Minds at the University of Wisconsin-Madison.

"Why is it that certain people are vulnerable to life's slings and arrows and why are other people more resilient?"

This question led Dr. Davidson into his field of research and expertise. He was curious as to why some people could handle life better than others, and he wanted to know if there were ways to learn from those who are resilient. Then maybe he could instill these qualities in those who lack the trait.

**

During the 2000 Mind & Life conference, Richard Davidson had a pivotal moment with His Holiness the Dalai Lama. The Dalai Lama rightfully points out in our culture (the Western culture) "We've been using tools of modern neuroscience to study depression, anxiety, and fear. Why can't we use those same tools to study kindness and compassion?"

Why not study kindness and compassion?

Simple question, difficult answer. Like most people, Dr. Davidson did not have a very good explanation for why he wasn't looking at the positive traits of mind other than that it was hard. However, in the words of Davidson, "This was a wakeup call." This conversation has reoriented Davidson's entire life, giving him a purpose. As he puts it, "I feel like I'm on this planet today to do this."

The Dalai Lama wanted to present meditation in a way that would be accessible to everyone and anyone. People cannot be deprived of this wonderful technique just based on the circumstances of their birth or other outside forces. So this was part of Dr. Davidson's task as he set out to study meditation, a path that most scholars of the time would say was a waste of a good Ph.D.

**

It turns out that the networks in our brains are frequently changing. Back to the idea that our brains stop changing at 20 and then we are forever living with the mind of a college student—well this idea is, to use a scientific term, "bull shit."

There is an idea in the scientific community called neuroplasticity. It refers to the ability of neurons to change in form and function in response to shifts in their environment. In other words, you have the ability to change the networks in your brain, the way you react, the way you think. You are in control of how you respond to every situation, and this response can change with experience.

This study, while on the surface may seem self-explanatory, was groundbreaking. It provides a basis for our ability as humans to change how we react.

I am someone who often struggles with traffic. Whenever I found myself stuck in unexpected traffic, it would drive me crazy! I would feel my grip unconsciously tighten on the wheel. I could feel the anger coursing through my body, just waiting to scream at the first stranger who cut me off or honked at me. No one wronged me in this situation, I was not mad at any one specifically; rather it was the image of traffic that triggered my anger. This is my associative network running at full speed: I see traffic and immediately my brain thinks anger. But what if I could change this? Perhaps I could sense I was getting angry, take a deep breath, and tell myself that I cannot control traffic and that being angry does nothing but hurt me. The more I do this, the less my brain associates traffic with anger and eventually, traffic will arise and I will be naturally at ease without having to tell myself it is going to be okay.

Obviously, we all have certain traits that we are born with and habits that we have formed so each one of us will have a different personality, a different way of reacting to situations, but we are by no means fixed in these ways. If there is something that you want to change, you truly have the power to do it. It frees human beings from feeling stuck in habits and actions that have hindered them for years.

As you can imagine, this provides a sturdy backbone for many of the claims coming out of the meditation community: decreasing stress, anxiety, depression; increasing happiness, compassion; rapid healing of the physical body. If we put this research into context, it allows us to see, and ultimately change many of our mental states.

\*\*

"Why is it that certain people are vulnerable to life's slings and arrows and why are other people more resilient?" Back to the question that was Davidson's driving force behind all of this research on meditation.

Davidson realized early on that each human being is unique, that each person has his or her own emotional makeup—we all know this to be true as our emotional responses often differ, even if only slightly, from those around us. It is this individuality that explains one person's ability to enjoy life's roller coaster and why another finds this roller coaster to be a terror-filled ride and desperately wants to get off.

Davidson also spent much of his career surrounded by some remarkable people. These were people like the Dalai Lama, who are not known just for their academic or professional achievements but are even more famous for their demeanor. These individuals have a positive outlook on the world, and an ability to regulate their emotional responses.

When you combine the science with the people and add in neuroplasticity:

1. **The individuality of people's emotional makeup** – the idea that every person has a unique emotional response, one that has been refined and cemented into a habit over the years.
2. **The remarkable people who have an incredible demeanor** – people like the Dalai Lama who can react from a place of kindness and compassion in every situation. Even when His Holiness was forced to flee Tibet due to Chinese occupation, he did not wish harm on the Chinese and refused to engage in any political actions, such as sanctions, that would cause suffering for the Chinese people.
3. **Neuroplasticity** – the constant ability for our neural networks to change and connect in new ways.

When you combine all these, you can see that a person has the capacity to change their emotional makeup, to respond from a place of kindness like the Dalai Lama. We can see that this ability is not innate nor only reserved for people like His Holiness, but rather it can be taught, it can be learned, and it can be achieved in our lifetime. Davidson knew that there was this potential, but now he needed to prove how to do it.

Cue meditation.

He wanted to see if meditation could have any impact on our ability to regulate emotional states. Davidson put a group of people through an 8-week Mindfulness Based Stress Reduction course. He took a group of people who had never meditated before had them work through basic mindfulness and meditation techniques, asking the participants to meditate for about twenty minutes a day.

Running a diagnostic after the 8 weeks, Dr. Davidson and his team saw a notable increase in the participant's abilities to regulate their emotions. He recorded that the participants who had undergone the MBSR course reported feeling much happier. Yet nothing had changed for these participants other than the addition of a few minutes of daily meditation. They worked at the same job, had the same relationships, and faced the same personal struggles, yet they overwhelmingly felt happier.

This information when compared to a control group was enough to assert the claim: meditation gives us control over our emotional states. This in no way means that these participants are without emotions, on the contrary, they have found a greater ability to respond with the desired emotion in the current situation, similar to the demeanor of His Holiness the Dalai Lama.

**

When I tell most people that meditation has not only profound mental effects but also profound physical effects, they often look at me as if I am some crazy person preaching alternative medicine, telling them that instead of Advil, they should hop on one foot to get rid of a headache. Or, rather, they should sit quietly and meditate.

Want to know a secret? It actually works!

I used to get sick all the time. I remember during my freshman year of college, I was sick with a cold for practically the entire year. Even if it was just residual sniffles and a cough, it was as if I would bounce from sickness to sickness, never able to get over the original virus. I tried everything. Advil, stronger medication, super complex multi-vitamins, a Chinese herb that promised I would get better, but none of this worked. The medicine did nothing to prevent me from getting sick so frequently.

Since I started my daily meditation practice, I am rarely sick. You may be questioning this assertion so I am going to explain what I think is happening. My meditation practice has helped me mentally. It has helped me overcome some states of anxiety and depression, mental states that can have a huge physical impact. Did you know that a depressed mental state has the ability to weaken your immune system? Depression among other things weakens your ability to fight off disease.[17] So by helping to enliven my mental states of mind, I was able to create a positive physical impact.

Most people do not know that meditation has an impact on one's physical being. Not just because I am saying it, but because scientists have managed to find support for this fact.

In another one of Dr. Davidson's early experiments, he set out to prove that meditation has some effect on the body's physical health. He set up an experiment to give two groups of people a flu vaccine—a flu vaccine is a really a small dose of the flu, with the goal being to familiarize your body for the virus. Group 1 consisted of people who had recently undergone an 8-week MBSR course and Group 2 was a control group who had never meditated before.

In this experiment, they saw that the meditators had a better immune response. By tracking the levels of antibodies produced by the immune systems of these individuals, Dr.

---

17  Legg, Tim, Ann Pietrangelo, and Kristen Cherney. 2017. "The Effects Of Depression In Your Body". *Healthline.*

Davidson was able to compare the groups. The data showed more antibodies in people who had meditated, proving that their bodies were better equipped to respond to the virus. Remember this is not an experiment comparing monks to a control group, rather this is a group of people who had never been exposed to meditation 8 weeks prior to this experiment.

I know what you might be thinking, these participants were only administered a flu vaccine, something that most of us willingly get every year to help prevent the flu. Well, another individual is a science experiment himself. His name is Wim Hof, and he along with 12 of his trainees took this hypothesis to the next level, proving the impact that the mind can have on the body.

The world knows Wim Hof as the Iceman. He got this eccentric title from the 21 world records he holds, almost all of them involving ice. He has the record running a marathon above the Arctic Circle barefoot, wearing nothing but shorts. He has another for the longest swim under the ice (66 meters).[18] Wim Hof has achieved some incredible feats that have defied what everyone thought the human body could do. When asked how, Wim says, "What I am capable of, everyone can learn."

---

18 Hof, W. 2018. "The History Of The 'Iceman' Wim Hof." *Wim Hof Method*.

Wim Hof has found a way to use breathing techniques and his mind to gain greater control over his central nervous system. This is what allows him to remain submerged in ice for over an hour without his internal body temperature dropping one degree.

This puzzles scientists. They have not been able to understand how this man could be defying what they thought were the limits of human nature. They wanted to put Wim to the ultimate test. In a controlled experiment, Wim Hof and 12 individuals that he trained were administered endotoxin, a dead cell wall component of bacteria. The body believes that endotoxin is live bacteria and creates the like-kind immune response, leaving the body with flu-like symptoms (chills, fever, headaches and more).

Wim received endotoxin while practicing meditation and breathing techniques. Measuring some key immune response metrics, scientists found that Wim's immune response was significantly different from other healthy patients who had undergone the same experiment. Wim's immune response was 50% less than that of healthy participants and he experienced no flu-like symptoms. It would appear as though, Wim was able to control his immune system, a feat that science had yet to measure. Further, to dispel all doubts about the capacity to do this, Wim trained 12 individuals who all underwent the same experiment. All of his trainees saw the same response, showing no symptoms associated with the administration of the bacteria.

Wim Hof has been able to show the mind's capacity to control the body, portraying the mind's true power.

**

These are incredible studies and some of my personal favorites because they highlight meditation in an environment that is physically focused. In a time where everyone is striving for physical fitness and well-being, these studies show that meditation has a true place not only in strengthening our mind but also our bodies.

Also now I can tell people that I feel significantly better since I started meditating, which I do, and have scientific support to prove it. Meditation teacher, Dr. Home Nguyen, hasn't taken an Advil in 20 years, for every time he gets a headache, he can use meditation to ease the pain. Incredible!

## DR. JUDSON BREWER

*"We need to understand how the mind works, then we can use any platform to help be a learning tool."*

— DR. JUDSON BREWER

Dr. Judson Brewer is a pioneer in the meditation community. Over the past few years, he has established himself as a thought leader in the field of habit change. He is working to teach people the "science of self-mastery", combining over 20 years of experience in mindfulness with scientific research. You might remember Dr. Brewer from Chapter Four; he focuses on the brain's ability to form habits and how forming habits, both good and bad, affects your life. In his research, he has deconstructed the brains hardwiring and has found a use for meditation practices in helping people overcome anxiety, addiction and much more.

\*\*

Dr. Brewer got into meditation through his own experience with suffering. He describes being stressed as a college graduate who was getting ready to embark on the journey that is medical school. He was doing well in school and had a college sweetheart who he planned to propose to. Overall, he had a plan for the foreseeable future. On the surface, his life looked great but when he dug a little deeper, he realized this mountain of stress underneath the tip of the iceberg. I think most us can relate to this feeling.

As medical school approached, Dr. Brewer found that he was having trouble sleeping. To make matters worse, the relationship with his fiancée ended and they were both heading to the same school. So if he couldn't sleep before, imagine the mental toll that an experience like this has on someone in their 20s. He was going through a period of great change and dealing with that is hard enough for anyone.

Judson started meditating the first day of medical school. As his journey from college graduate to doctorate progressed, he kept up with his practice. Meditation was an excellent side hobby. Judson was reaping the benefits of meditation like increased concentration and reduced anxiety while still being able to focus on his studies in molecular biology. The meditation provided an anchor that grounded him during this high-stress period.

10 years had passed since the first time Judson sat down to try and watch his breath enter and leave his body, but he had not yet transitioned studying the science of meditation, he had not yet combined his work and passion. This, however, would all change as Judson began to question what was happening on a neurological level. What do our brains do as we meditate?

**\*\***

"Seeing clearly what the mental processes are," this is Dr. Brewer's definition of mindfulness. He wants to show people the power of the mind, saying that in order to comprehend what we can do with this incredible gift, we need to first understand how it works. His goal is to educate people about their minds and how they function, asking people to just get curious and have a desire to learn— for with knowledge comes power.

After pivoting away from molecular biology, Dr. Brewer started to focus on meditation from both a psychological and neurological standpoint. He has used tools like meditation and mindfulness to help people quit smoking, to help people give up their dependence on alcohol or drugs, and to help people overcome cravings and other issues with food.

Earlier in the book (Chapter Four), I presented Dr. Brewer's theory, that our brains function on habit loops or the desire to reinforce good feelings and avoid negative ones. As conscious beings gifted with the power of thought, we were also given this mode of thinking, these habit loops. A habit loop, while it can be a good thing, is often a reinforcer of things that are bad for us. For example, if we pick up the habit of smoking in hopes of reducing anxiety then we will start to associate smoking with the reduction of anxiety and every time we feel anxious we want to smoke.

Given all of the research that is out there, almost everyone who smokes knows it is bad for them, and many people try to quit. The problem is that the habit is so ingrained that even those who want to give it up simply cannot. They try to stop smoking and before they know it, they find themselves with another cigarette in their mouths. Habit loops are extremely powerful and very difficult to overcome.

This idea is also applicable to food cravings, or the desire to eat something when we are not actually hungry—most often we are not reaching for a salad but rather that bag of chips or something sweet (or both). During these moments, this same habit loop is being activated. We feel a negative feeling and our body's response is to remind us how good a piece of cake tastes in hopes of making us feel better. Unfortunately, even when the cake tastes great, we are usually more upset afterward. We know that we didn't want to eat that cake right now, yet it all happened so fast, and before we even knew it, we eat our second, third, fourth maybe even fifth piece.

This is Dr. Brewer's focus. He tries to show that meditation is a tool that can drive a wedge of awareness in those ingrained habit loops.

**

I signed up for one of his 7-day email courses. The goal of this course was "understanding cravings," helping people like me work through difficult eating habits. One of the days, we did a body scan exercise. For a refresher on a body scan, you can refer back to Chapter Six, but in short, this exercise entails lying or sitting down and trying to bring awareness to every part of your body a little bit at a time. You start with your left foot and try to be aware of the sensations and feelings in the toes on the left foot and slowly progress all the way up to the top of your head.

The aim of the exercise in this context was to try to find where in the body one holds cravings. Asking us to think about our favorite foods, Dr. Brewer was trying to help simulate the body's reaction to a craving. This can be a number of feelings, but for me, it is often that feeling that I might explode if I do not eat that food immediately.

The body scan helps create comfortability with the sensations that are present. It helped me recognize that cravings are nothing but some strong sensations in the body. As I went through the practice, I would find some tightness in certain places. When I would think about that piece of chocolate cake that I wanted, I could feel the response in my body. I could watch as my chest would tighten, producing a feeling so discomforting that I felt like I might explode if I did not get my cake. However, the more I sat, the more the feelings dispersed. The tightness in my chest started to loosen and after a few minutes of sitting, I no longer wanted the cake.

As I slowly devoted attention to different limbs and muscles, I started to regain control over my body and mind allowing me to see the cravings and not allow them to pull me. Simply by sitting with this feeling for a few minutes, the craving started to dissipate.

I can personally attest to the effectiveness of this exercise and I continue to use it when I find myself mindlessly reaching for the bag of chips or my favorite desserts. On top of my personal testimony, Dr. Brewer's research has shown that mindfulness techniques can lead to a 40% reduction in eating issues, a 50% reduction in anxiety and 5 times more quit rates in smokers when compared to leading methods of therapy.

It is such a simple concept yet it is so profound at the same time. We are in control of how we act, what we do. Yet our minds are powerful enough to take this control away from us, to hijack us. This is what a habit loop does. By simply trying to regain control, to take a step back and see that someone else, something else is in command, it can help us to break these habits that have held us back for so long.

If you are someone who has a bad habit that you have been unable to break, give meditation a try. You do not need to sit down for 40 minutes a day or anything. Rather as Dr. Brewer says, "It is better to try and be mindful for a few seconds than to meditate for 40 minutes and be a jerk for the rest of the day."

So give it a try.

Get curious and see what is going on in your mind.

## PUSHING PAST SCIENCE

Science is not the end all be all for meditators. I would highly doubt that most people sit on a pillow every morning and think: "I am doing this because I might see a reduction in my cortisol levels and therefore reduce the amount of stress in my life, which will stop the telomeres on the ends of my chromosomes from degrading as rapidly ultimately extending my life."

If this is the main driver of your meditation, then please do not stop, keep doing you. But if you are like me and many others that I have talked to, then you know that the science is interesting but it is not the stable flooring that our practice needs.

When I asked Dr. Brewer if he thought the scientific findings had a profound impact on people practicing he said, "These concepts are like sugar, they provide empty calories that just get us jonesing for more… we need to drop down into the body in order to find the real meat."

The scientific findings are incredible, and they are very captivating and much like a delicious sugary treat, we like them a lot. Unfortunately, sugary treats cannot sustain us in the long run, just like simple scientific knowledge cannot sustain our meditation practices.

Ultimately, even if you are skeptical, this practice is worth a try. It is in the effort of practicing that you will find the real reason you are sitting, your true motivation for being present. The science will simply become an interesting fact to spark the conversation.

# CHAPTER 12

# FINDING BALANCE, MEDITATING THROUGH LIFE'S UPS AND DOWNS

---

Meditation is much more than just a practice.

For some people, it can become a way of life. For others it can provide deep and profound insights. It may even become something that defines you and in rare cases, it might save your life.

**

Phakyab Rinpoche sought refuge in New York in April of 2003. He was immediately hospitalized for severe gangrene in his right foot. Phakyab had been tortured in Chinese occupied Tibet, once his home country, now his place of capture.

Phakyab, as he puts it, had been "reduced to the despicable dregs of society with a dismantled body dismembered by torture." When the doctors received Phakyab Rinpoche they believed that an amputation was necessary, that there would be no way to save the foot and have him survive.

Those were his choices, amputate or risk death.

This was not Phakyab's wish. Like anyone, he did not want to lose his leg.

Seeking help, Phakyab reached out to his friend and guide, His Holiness the Dalai Lama.

"Why are you looking for healing outside of you? You have wisdom in you that heals, and once healed, you will teach the world how to heal."

This was His Holiness' response.

## AN INSIGHT PRACTICE

Insight – the capacity to gain an accurate and deep intuitive understanding.[19]

Meditation provides self-insight.

Meditation asks you to be present, but as we have discussed it doesn't ask you to shut off your thoughts. It is completely natural for the brain to think, and meditation is no exception to this norm. This is where the insight comes in.

If you have ever had a clogged drain in your house, you would know that eventually, the drain reaches its capacity. There becomes a blockage, and nothing can flow through.

This is analogous to our minds.

We constantly shove things down the drain of our mind – thoughts about school, work, parties, family, friends, TV, and more. Every input that we have, every thought that we think, this all flows through the drain of our minds. For a while, it can flow naturally, as we make our way through life. Nevertheless, sometimes we can have a blockage, often a traumatic or an emotional thought that disrupts the flow. Now it might not be enough to stop the drain completely,

---

19  "Insight." *Google Dictionary.*

but it can certainly cause difficulty. We start struggling to deal with more intense inputs, defaulting to TV over reading a book, or eating over doing our work. We choose things that don't require our brain to expend too much effort.

Finally, it gets overwhelming. The drain of our mind gets completely blocked and we shut down. Some of us react by breaking down and crying, others lash out with strong emotions, some might even give up completely.

The point is all of us get overwhelmed. We reach a point where we simply cannot handle any more input and things start to bubble back up.

What if you could stop this before it happened?

You can.

The answer is to have a plumber come and take a look when the drain isn't flowing well. He or she will be able to dislodge the blockage and you won't have to worry about your kitchen sink overflowing and flooding your house.

Meditation is the mind's plumber.

Yes, I know this is a very sexy analogy and makes meditation seem super cool, but it really is a great description. You see, meditation allows you to confront the blockage before it gets to the point of overflowing, flooding your mind with negativity. It allows you to see what is going on in your head, your body, and your life before all of the thoughts, feelings, emotions and more overwhelm you. When you see this, you can proactively take care of the problems.

This is why meditation is an insight practice, for it can truly give you insight into yourself providing you the space to make a change.

**

After hearing the advice of the Dalai Lama, Phakyab Rinpoche took to meditation immediately. He refused the amputation, found a temporary place to live, and started a 12-hour-a-day meditation practice stopping only to eat, sleep, and use the bathroom. The doctors believed this was a death sentence. Phakyab thought otherwise as he began to look inside himself. He engaged in a unique concentration practice called *tsa lung* where he would imagine a purifying wind clearing out all of the channels in his body. He would sit there for hours, just focusing on this wind, imagining that he could use this force to rid him of his injuries, to save his life.

However, despite his effort, Phakyab's leg began to get worse. It started to ooze black liquid and puss. Shortly afterward, his leg began to bruise and swell becoming increasingly painful. On top of that, there was a foul smell. It was as if his leg was slowly decaying while he was still alive. Yet he continued to meditate. Even with the pain, he still continued to sit the 12 hours and imagine a metaphysical wind clearing his body.

## SHINING A FLASHLIGHT

Meditation shines a flashlight into the dark corners of your mind.

This is a common expression in Western Buddhism.

Yes, meditation provides insight, but for some insight is not a pleasant feeling. Insight can be overwhelming in its own way, as it can remind us all of the things we are avoiding thinking about. Those things start to come up in our practice and they start to stay on our minds always.

What type of things could we be avoiding?

Often these are difficult emotional issues, traumas and other states of mind that we dislike. Usually, this is the stuff that would "clog" the "drain" of your mind.

Trying to confront difficult thoughts and emotions is no easy task to deal with, but one cannot figure out the solution before the problem is known. Meditation helps us to see these problems and it gives us the ability to understand and eventually overcome them.

**

Nine months after starting this 12-hour daily practice, Phakyab Rinpoche's leg started to heal. His swelling started to retreat the smell started to fade. Shortly afterward he began walking again using crutches. And, after about a year he could walk again on his own.

Phakyab Rinpoche did the impossible. He managed to reverse the gangrene that was attacking his leg, a process for which modern medicine had no answer. He saved his leg and his life. A truly astonishing achievement, and one that doctors are still trying to understand.

Phakyab Rinpoche managed to use meditation to effect a physical change and save his life.

**

I am not saying that meditation will do the same for us, but the thought is no longer impossible. The lesson here is that meditation can allow you to access innate power and deep understanding within you. I will most likely never physically heal myself through meditation, but mentally, I have made strides greater than I could've ever imagined.

## YAEL SHY

*"This practice puts you back in yourself, it doesn't take you somewhere else."*

— YAEL SHY

Yael Shy is an author and the head of Global Spiritual Life at New York University. She works every day to help provide the techniques and tools of meditation and mindfulness to her students, showing them that they really don't have to be anything besides themselves.

Meditation does not solve all of your problems.

This is a common misconception for people when they start something like therapy, working out, or meditation. We expect one therapy session to eradicate all of our childhood trauma, or one day at the gym to get us the perfect body, or one meditation to lead immediately to enlightenment. We have expectations about how the world should work and when we do things that are difficult like therapy, fitness, and meditation, we expect to see benefits immediately.

I experienced a similar mindset when I began my practice. I remember thinking, "Okay, so I will sit for a few minutes and when I get up I will feel incredible, I will be able to understand myself completely and shortly thereafter I will be enlightened and all of my suffering will dissipate leaving me with the most perfect life."

I figured that it would just take a few sessions, and I could throw this thing to the side and live my best life. Somewhat how I thought I could work out for a few weeks and have the picture perfect 21st-century body. Three years of meditation later (and ten of working out), I can honestly say that I am living my best life. However, in no way have I reached my potential nor have I stopped meditating, or working out. Instead I have increased the time I spend on the cushion and in the gym, wanting to always learn more and find ways to be more present throughout the day.

When we look at meditation as a quick fix, we expect too much. It gives this idea that this one thing can solve all of your problems instantly and when this fantasy does not bear fruit, there will be a huge upset. Yes, meditation saved Phakyab Rinpoche but that took over 4,000 hours of practice in one year.

Meditation is a journey. Like most journeys, it is not so much about the destination but rather the process to get there. The beauty of meditation is in the practice itself. The practice of being present. This is the journey.

**

Anxiety has skyrocketed in our society. There are so many more pressures that we face on a daily basis. There is pressure to do well in school, pressure to partake in valuable extracurriculars, pressure to get into a good college, pressure to have a flourishing social life, pressure to drink and party, pressure to post on social media, pressure to partake in sexual activity, pressure to find love, pressure to get a good job – the list goes on and on with the need to constantly do more and be better. There are all of these "requirements" that society has created, and in order for us to feel good, we feel an overwhelming pressure to check all of these boxes.

We feel like we need to post on social media to show people incredible snippets of our world when what we are doing is really presenting a false view of our lives to others and often to ourselves. We may feel like we need to go out and get drunk when all we really want to do is stay in. We may feel pressured to pick up an activity just because it will look good on a resume. These things can actually control our lives.

Add to that the current state of the world, the worries of a global war, or another recession. The worry that you might not be able to get a job after college, or keep your current job. All of these external fears start to blend with the internal to cause a pressure cooker, a volcano of anxiety that is heading toward eruption.

**

"During my junior year of college at New York University, I ducked into a clothing store on Broadway and Thirteenth to find some quiet as I dialed my friend Sasha. 'I can't breathe again,' I said in short gusts, as my chest constricted. I felt lightheaded and dizzy, and I was covered in a cold sweat. I was having a panic attack—my third that month."[20]

This is an excerpt from Yael Shy's book, *What Now: Meditation for your Twenties and Beyond.* In it, she talks about the stress and anxiety she felt as a college student and continues to manage today. She describes having continuous breakdowns and panic attacks, episodes of pure anxiety that she could not control.

With an incredible openness, she details the struggles that she went through, struggles that can be found in almost all of us.

---

20 What Now, Meditation for your Twenties and Beyond → Shy, Y. 2017. *What Now?: Meditation for your Twenties and Beyond.* California: Parallax Press.

The constant bouts with panic became more frequent for Yael as the year progressed. Most people assume that college kids are stressed about school and homework but often forget that students deal with things like finding true love, feeling like they don't belong, trying to bridge the gap between child and adult, struggling to pay for their education and so much more. Yael was a student in New York right after 9/11. So on top of all of the internal struggles, she was scared of her external environment. That is enough to send anyone into panic and most college kids do not seek help. The American Disability Association found that 85% of college students reported feeling overwhelmed by everything they had to do, and while the number of those individuals seeking mental health has grown, it is still not enough.[21] So many of us are walking around anxious and stressed with no end in sight, no idea how to ease these feelings.

After a few more really bad panic episodes, Yael Shy decided to go on a silent meditation retreat. On this retreat, recommended to her by her mom, Yael found herself sitting on the cushion in a room with a bunch of other practitioners. She expected a few days of nice relaxation, but instead, she found her anxiety bubbling up. She wasn't at all relaxed – in fact, the experience was the opposite of that.

---

21 "Mental Health and College Students." *Anxiety and Depression Association of America.*

Midway through the retreat, Yael got the opportunity to speak with one of the teachers. It was the first time she had spoken in days. She recounts, breaking down, letting all of her fears, all of her anxiety, pour out. Her fear of loneliness, of not being loved, of dying; fears that all of us have but often do not confront. All of these started to emerge on this meditation retreat. Now, the lid was off the top, the volcano had erupted, but the lava wasn't as scary as she thought. The more she started to look at these fears, the less scary they became.

Meditation can shine a light in the dark corners of our minds. This can often be something we are adverse to, scared of what the light may reveal. But those dark corners, the fears, the anxiety we never bring up, these feelings hate the light too and the more we shine it the more they begin to fade. Fear does not like being brought to the surface, and when you can stare it straight in the eye, it starts to lose its power over you.

Meditation did not save Yael Shy, it did not stop her anxiety, but it did help her to see her own self more clearly. This process has allowed her to gain greater control, a greater ability to regulate these difficult mental states. So while she still experiences moments of anxiety, she does not let them control her any longer.

**

This is what a great number of people seek to find. We want to alleviate our suffering, to gain more clarity, to experience something real.

Yael went on to work in the field of meditation, as the head of Global Spiritual Life at New York University, working to help students access this practice. Most of her students and even adults that she works with are looking for the same thing, the potential to alleviate suffering.

No one is immune.

No matter how old you are, how smart you are, what your upbringing was, we all must confront suffering. We will all deal with the difficulties that life throws at us. We will go through stress and turmoil and fight our way to make it out on the other side.

If you can remember our definition of suffering from Chapter One, suffering is often just attachment. We all have attachments, we all want things, people and states of mind. We would all rather be in a happy state of mind than a sad one. Further, we often cling to this happiness, not wanting it to end. While meditation doesn't rid us of our problems or our attachments, it gives us the power to decide when to let things go. It shows us that we do not need to cling to attachments, that we do not need to let our wants and desires become an object of suffering. We can still have wants and be okay with the present moment as it is.

Meditation teaches us how to do just that. Mediation can help us figure out what is real and realize the differences between our reality and the suffering that we create. Meditation gives us deeper insight, and with that insight, we become the guide of our lives.

Meditation is the compass, we are the guide, and the present moment is where we are heading.

## SHARON SALZBERG

Sharon Salzberg is an incredibly influential figure in the world of meditation. After returning from India in 1971, Sharon helped to found the Insight Meditation Society, which is one of the most prominent and active meditation centers in the Western world. She is also a meditation teacher and an author of many incredible books like *Lovingkindness* and New York Times bestseller, *Real Happiness*. In her work, she emphasizes the importance of spreading love and kindness to the world, an endeavor with which she has had great success.Sharon Salzberg was a sophomore in college when she applied for a grant to travel to India. She had taken an Asian Philosophy class and was intrigued by the material. The idea of meditation and how it could help alleviate suffering was something she was drawn to immediately.

Sharon had an extremely difficult childhood. Her parents divorced when she was only four. Her father abandoned the family shortly thereafter. At age 9, Sharon's mother died. She was sent to live with her father's parents. Her father came back into the picture when she was 11, but he was hospitalized for a drug overdose and then placed in a mental care facility until his death. By the age of 16, Sharon had already lived with five different families. She was well-versed in suffering.

In 1967, Sharon was admitted into SUNY Buffalo. It was here that she fell in love with Buddhism, with the idea of learning how to overcome and possibly escape from her own suffering. It was here that she was able to apply for an independent study program and travel to India in order to learn from some incredible teachers, but most of all, she learned how to teach herself, how to learn continuously from the experiences that she faced.

Often in our experiences, we tend to add commentary to the events of our day. Have you ever walked by a familiar face, said "hello" and the person either does not say "hi" back or clearly doesn't recognize you? This is a very common occurrence on college campuses as you are constantly meeting new people. Regardless, if this has happened to you, you will remember how fast your mind starts to jump to conclusions. "Oh my god, this person must not think I am important enough to remember. She totally hates me. I am useless. No one likes me." This stream of thought can spiral out of control as we start to add on commentary to our experiences.

What actually happens in this situation is more likely the following: *you wave to the person* *He or she is lost in thought or dealing with some internal feelings. They are so caught up in themselves that their brain cannot put together your face and the recognition thereof, so they don't wave.* Odds are the lack of a response is a total accident; yet, we find a way not only to make it intentional but also to allow it to tear us down mentally.

Meditation allows us to differentiate. It allows us to see what is real and what is commentary that we add on to our own lives. With this knowledge, we can choose to live in reality, to live in what is actually happening and not be wrapped up in our minds, which, let's be honest, have the tendency to spiral downward.

Over the years, Sharon has slowly started to drive awareness into the difference between her commentary and reality. However, it is by no means easy. She still struggles with innate reactions, the body's programming taking over in these situations, but the more she practices, the more she is able to separate reality. Reality is not good or bad, it simply is. Our own commentary adds on this state of being good or more often bad.

## STRIVING FOR THE PRESENT

We have all had profound experiences, feelings of connection to something bigger and greater than ourselves. We don't live in this state very often, but we are all familiar with this notion: the moments when we are fully present, completely content with where we are. The moments where we realize that good and bad are things we create and reality cannot fall into either bucket. For Sharon, Yael, and many others, this is the goal of meditation. It is not about getting something, but about experiencing what we know to be something beautiful: the present moment as it is. It is not about going anywhere, but being okay with right here.

Meditation does not make the pain or suffering, go away, but it allows us to realize there is another side of the coin. We can see that happiness is out there for every one of us. Therefore, this is what we should continue to strive for: happiness, love, and kindness.

# PART IV

## LET'S DO THIS, JUMP-STARTING YOUR OWN JOURNEY

*"The thing about meditation is: You become more and more you."*

— DAVID LYNCH

Up until now, we have learned a lot about the practices and the people who do them, but this part is for you. This section aims at helping you go from A to B, to get from where you are now to where you want to be. This is a recipe for growth and success catered just to you.

Everyone learns in different ways, some people like sports or business analogies, others like information presented in actionable steps. Whatever your method of learning, the point is that no two people are the same. When I teach these practices to friends and family, I always put a different spin on a similar concept, choosing my words and explanations to best try to reach the person sitting across from me. This is what I am trying to do right now. I have broken the following chapters up into sections with the aim of reaching a wide range of readers. So, read all of them or just read what speaks to you, but use these as a jumping off point to help you grow, to help you adopt a practice or lay a foundation using the information below.

The Chapters:

- **Meditation for Athletes** – Someone who has been sports-focused their entire life and who would benefit from both practices that will better your athletic performance and language that speaks to the athlete in you. Whether you are a college or professional athlete, a gymaholic, or just a human being with a body there are some great takeaways here.

- **Mindful Leadership** – Someone who is career-focused, wants to be a leader in the world, and wants to know how meditation can fit into this plan. Learn about what it means to be a mindful leader and how you can do it, no matter what job or what role you are in.

- **The Skeptical Guru** – If you are still doubtful and skeptical in any way of meditation, if there is anything that turns you off or makes you feel as if meditation isn't for you, let me try to convince you otherwise. Whether it is religion, thinking meditation isn't cool enough, or worrying that you won't be good at it, this is the place for you.

- **Struggling Mindfully** – If life is not everything that you thought it would be, or if you just want skills to handle those rough patches, this is the place to go. There is nothing wrong with having low points in life, it is only natural. Here you can learn how to get out of your own way and overcome even those difficult times.

- **The Average Joe, Turned Meditation Professional** – If you have fallen in love with the ideas in this book or you already know that you want to take your practice to the next level, these are some tips on how to do it. Whether it is trying to establish a daily practice or wanting to teach others, this is your one-stop shop.

**

These chapters are all organized in the same way.

Each chapter starts with a quote from a meditation practitioner that I have interviewed during my journey. All the quotes are answers to the same question:

*Knowing everything you know now, what advice would you give to your college-age self?*

The goal is to frame the chapter, by having you reflect on what these experts have to say, what advice they would give to themselves and by proxy all of us. The chapters then dive into the best practices for helping you grow in whatever field you are interested in, working to give you personalized practices and ideas to help you build and develop your meditation practice.

Each chapter then ends with a quote from a college-aged individual. Similar to how the chapter started, these individuals are all answering the following question:

*What advice would you give to yourself right now?*

These individuals are "friends of mind," people that I have taught meditation to, people who are taking the time to meditate, to think about their lives and to find ways that they can better themselves. Their advice is given to themselves, but it is also something from which we can derive value. Use these quotes to think about where you are right now and where you want to go. Let the words of others be a guide for you as you begin your journey.

By reading this book, you too have become a "friend of mind," and you too must learn how to use all of this material for you. After you finish reading, there is a special section reserved for you on the final page of this book. Just like everyone I have quoted in here, you will be asked the same question:

*What advice would you give to yourself right now?*

Let the answer to this question solidify your practice. By putting this into words, you are taking the first step toward growth, you are solidifying your desire to live by this advice and positioning yourself to take on the world.

*"Be a guiding light, a light that has the power to change the world, to effect change simply by being. Though I may not shine the brightest, at the end of the day I must be me and you must be you, but together we can light up the entire world."*

— ANDREW FEINSTEIN, ADVICE TO HIMSELF

# CHAPTER 13

# MEDITATION FOR ATHLETES

———

*"This stuff can change your life and trajectory."*

— GRAHAM BETCHART, *AUTHOR OF PLAY PRESENT, A MENTAL SKILLS TRAINING PROGRAM FOR BASKETBALL PLAYERS*

Nike co-founder Bill Bowerman says, "If you have a body, you are an athlete." I believe the same. You don't have to be a hall of fame athlete, or a 7-day a week gym-goer, rather you can be just who you are and still be an athlete. It is all about how you look at yourself.

Athletes are not foreign to the concepts found within meditation and mindfulness. As many athletes have heard, "80% of the game is mental," but what does that actually mean? An athlete has spent his or her entire life training, they have perfected the hard skills, and now the only thing standing in the way is the mind.

Some would argue that your opponent is the biggest obstacle, but you cannot control your opponent. You can, however, gain greater control over your own mind, or at least have it stop being an obstacle.

At one point in my life, I was training to be a competitive boxer. I remember one of the first things my trainer told me after my first sparring session was that the hardest obstacle to overcome in that ring was not the guy trying to hit me, but it was actually me. He explained that if I can control my breathing and my emotions then I can react to my opponent. I can control the outcome of the fight by controlling my awareness, not by controlling my opponent.

This same sentiment is echoed in the newest movie in the Rocky Series, *Creed*. At one point during the training montage, Rocky (Sylvester Stallone) has Adonis (Michael B. Jordan) stand in front of the mirror. Having Adonis stare back at himself in the mirror, Rocky says, "This guy right here, that's the toughest opponent you are going to face..." You are the only obstacle standing in the way. When you start to get worried about your performance, you start to doubt your abilities; that is what leads to defeat.

This idea is not found just in boxing. Take golf for example, a sport where you are not directly competing against another player. There is no one trying to hit you back, or someone trying to block your shot, rather you hit your ball and then your opponent hits theirs. The match is totally in the hands of the player, yet you see top performing professionals fall apart, unable to make shots that they have been able to hit perfectly in the past. This is a clear instance of the mind getting in the way. An example of how worrying about making a good shot results in a bad shot...the dreaded self-fulfilling prophecy, or should I say self-defeating prophecy.

**

Graham Betchart in his book *Play Present: Mental Skills Training Program for Basketball Players* has created a playbook for the mindful athlete. This incredibly insightful, easy to read, life guide, teaches athletes how to be in the moment and trust in their skills.

Betchart works closely with George Mumford and together they have trained athletes like Michael Jordan, Kobe Bryant, Brandon Marshall, Aaron Gordon, BJ Penn, and many others.

These high performing athletes are still just people. They deal with the same stresses of life – the ups and downs that every person on this planet experiences. On top of this, they are also put under a microscope with their every action analyzed by the entire world.

Often athletes are so hyper-focused on creating success for themselves (on "making it") that they often do not take care of themselves. They miss out on this piece of training, of strengthening the mind, finding it a waste of time rather than an asset.

But just like you would train each muscle group and each skill for the sport you play, you need to train your mind. You need to create the conditions to be mentally prepared to face the challenges that come your way.

## ADMITTING YOUR WEAKNESS

Often players are told to stick to their strengths. For example, if you are a big man like Shaquille O'Neal, you should use your strength and size in the paint rather than shooting 3s. In MMA, if you are a better stand up puncher you would want to stay away from letting the match go to the ground. If you're a frequent gym goer but hate leg day, you would have a strong upper body and toothpick legs.

In sports and in life, avoiding the things we are bad at is a natural tendency; it is a way for us to avoid putting our weaknesses on display. If the match was on the line and you as a golfer aren't good with a driver, you would tee off with an iron and play it safe knowing you would need an extra shot rather than risk it. Or back to the dreaded "leg day," you would forego an important exercise, one that can help you to achieve your gym goals just because it is harder for you.

What we fail to realize is that by playing to our strengths, we build our weaknesses. Instead of learning to overcome these shortfalls, we let them fester until finally the game is on the line and we play it safe rather than going for it all. We are afraid to lose, we are afraid to show weakness.

Here is a word that is not used often in sports: **Vulnerability.**

In sports and in life, it is important to be vulnerable, to be willing to look your weaknesses directly in the face and say, "You cannot hold me back." Instead of refusing to make mistakes, we need to be okay with failing in order ultimately to succeed.

## FAILURE IS GOOD

*"I've missed more than 9000 shots in my career. I've lost almost 300 games. Twenty-six times, I've been trusted to take the game winning shot and missed. I've failed over and over and over again in my life. And that is why I succeed."*

— MICHAEL JORDAN

This quote by Michael Jordan, which we first saw in Chapter Five, summarizes perfectly that failure has a place in our lives. It not something that we should avoid. To bring back another quote, "Failure is just multiple iterations at success." In failure, we are simply laying the foundation to eventually succeed.

You cannot let failure get you down. Do not think that you aren't good enough, or there is no way that you will possibly accomplish the task in front of you. Failure is good, if you can accept and grow from it.

In order to make a huge leap forward, we need to take several steps back. In order to jump over a big chasm, you need a running start. Sometimes you need to go backward in order to eventually advance forward.

This analogy gives failure a purpose; it shows that failure is just a step back, creating room for a big leap forward, a leap to success. In order to succeed we need to fail.

## VISUALIZATIONS

Visualizations are the practice of imagining the thing that you want to happen. For instance, if as a basketball player you want to increase your ability to hit 3-point shots, it would be helpful to think about and visualize this process. It may sound a little silly, but actually, sit and picture the motion, try and see yourself from an outside perspective. Watch yourself catch the ball, bring it up to your ear, jump, and release. Try and see the full motion, picking out the key points where you need to pay more attention, the points in the shot where you might be rushing or shortcutting your form. Picture what it would take to make the ball go into the net.

While this activity may seem like a waste of time, it can help us to see what we need to work on. Once we see it then we can start to act on it.

This practice is also utilized in the world of boxing. One of the biggest elements to any boxer's training is shadow boxing. This is the art of punching the air, or your shadow, which as you can guess is the reason for the name. The purpose of this is to pretend and visualize that you are actually fighting someone else. Unlike just hitting a bag, this practice allows you to visualize your reactions and angles to the invisible opponent. By picturing your opponent throw a hook, you can roll underneath his or her punch countering with a left uppercut and an overhand right, change your angle and attack again with another flurry of punches.

When I would engage in the practice of shadow boxing, I would always see my shortcomings. I would notice when I wouldn't extend my jab all the way, or I would notice when my feet would cross and I would lose my balance. If I wasn't able to throw punches properly while fighting the air, how did I expect to fair in the ring against a real opponent. I used this practice to help make corrections, to hone in on my muscle memory and perfect my form.

Whether it is boxing, basketball, or just life, envisioning things in the right way helps create the right muscle memory.

## TRUST YOURSELF

Human beings are capable of amazing feats. As we have learned, we can rewire our brain constantly, and with that, we can create new and more ingrained muscle memories. This is how an athlete functions, they practice the same shot, the same punch, the same swing repeatedly until their body knows the motion in its sleep.

As a high performing athlete, you have trained your body to perform the perfect movements. You know how to make a strong cut on an out route in football. You know how hard to kick the ball in order to drill it in the top right corner of the net in soccer. You know when to release the ball in order to hear swish in basketball. You know how to make contact with the golf ball so it soars straight down the fairway. Whatever your sport is, you have practiced hundreds, thousands of times. You have put in hour after hour. You have given sweat, shed tears, and maybe even lost some blood. You have done all of this in preparation for this moment right in front of you.

When the game is on the line, who do you want to have the ball?

The answer: YOU.

You have trained for this and now all you have to do is trust yourself. Stop thinking about winning or losing, stop thinking that you are not good enough, stop worrying that you may fail. Focus on the present moment and trust your body.

## PLAYING PRESENT IN ACTION

Graham Betchart told me a story about one of the players he has helped coach, Aaron Gordon. For those who don't know, Aaron Gordon is the starting power forward for the

Orlando Magic. He just finished his 4th season in the NBA and is truly an electrifying player to watch.

There was a specific time in Gordon's 2016–2017 season where he had one of the worst games in his career. On December 1, 2016, Gordon and company took on the Grizzlies in Memphis, Tennessee. Gordon missed all of his 3-point shots, scored only eight points with three rebounds to lose the game 95–94.

"Look man, I'm going to be really real with you now and I don't see you doing it. I see you trying to play it safe," Graham Betchart said in the aftermath of this emotional defeat. Gordon was over thinking his game; he was worried about failing, worried about confronting his weaknesses.

Betchart told me that he and Gordon had been working on the 3-pointer for years now, as it was one of the vulnerable points of Gordon's game. Gordon was able to be vulnerable with Betchart in practice. He was able to say that he wanted to work on his 3-pointer and they did. They put endless time into it, using visualizations, breathing techniques and other mental practices to give Gordon the power to trust the process, to trust his form and just believe in his body.

Finally, the last thing holding him back was trusting himself. Gordon was capable of making the shots, but in this loss to Memphis, he was "playing it safe." Like the golfer taking the iron instead of the driver, Gordon got lost in the power of the mind, in the worry of failure rather than going for success. He just needed to play in the moment and trust his skills.

After this conversation with Betchart, Gordon went out to score a season-high of 20 points with two 3-pointers to beat the Philadelphia 76ers 105–88. Less than two weeks later, Gordon went on to score a career best of 33 points against the Clippers. After that, he lit up, posting 30 points in a rematch against Memphis later in the month, 22 against Carmelo Anthony and the Knicks, and 18 against James Harden and Rockets all ending in victories for the Magic.

Gordon managed to turn his game around almost instantaneously as he recalled the countless practice of turning down the volume of his mind. It was as if Graham Betchart gave him a pair of Michael Jordan's shoes, giving Gordon the same abilities that Lil' Bow Wow had in the movie *Like Mike*. However, Betchart didn't give Aaron Gordon anything material. Instead, Betchart just said what Gordon had heard for years but was still unable to believe: "You won't ever succeed if you aren't OK to fail."

That is the change that Gordon made. He was by no means perfect in the games that followed this conversation, but he was willing to miss shots, to make mistakes. He used his failures to create success. As Gordon puts it, "I'm OK now with seeing failure as a learning mechanism instead of just failure. You need to go through that fire to come out more polished. You need to go through the tough times to appreciate the good times. Honestly, it's helped me to see myself as more than a basketball player. Basketball is what I do, not who I am."

## CLEAR YOUR MIND, MAKE THE SHOT, WIN THE GAME

*"You're braver than you believe and stronger and smarter than you think."*

— WINNIE THE POOH.

Unlocking the power of the mind can truly help athletes everywhere. Just like I said in the beginning of the chapter, 80% of the game is mental, and most people are not harnessing that potential.

In a world where every athlete has the physical stamina and the skill, you need to find the leg up, you need to find your ability to play in the present and trust your body. You are capable of so much more than you know.

The game is on the line always, life will always throw you a curveball, and you might not have time to think about all of your options; you might just need to react. Trust that you can do it. Trust that you will either fail with grace or succeed beyond what you imagined.

*"Life will throw many distractions at you. Friends and strangers both will try to take your happiness, but that happiness is one of the few things that you can control. Never take anything personally, and always keep striving for your goals."*

— FRIEND OF MIND, AGE 22

# CHAPTER 14

# MINDFUL LEADERSHIP

———

*"Be attentive to 'how you want to be in the world' at least as much as 'what you want to do.'"*

— JANICE MARTURANO, *FOUNDER AND EXECUTIVE DIRECTOR OF THE INSTITUTE FOR MINDFUL LEADERSHIP*

Anyone can be a leader.

Think of a leader or someone who has had a profound influence on you. When you have this person in your mind, I want you to ask yourself one question. Why did this person come to mind, what is it about them that makes them a leader?

This is an exercise that Janice Marturano does in her course on mindful leadership. In all the times that she has asked this question not once has someone answered with "this person met quarterly earnings." Rather it is due to the person being "a good listener" or a "supporter," someone who makes you feel good, someone you can trust.

Leadership is not about the title that is next to your name. Rather, at its core, leadership is all about influence. A good leader is one who can influence those around them. A mindful leader is one who can take this a step further. As Janice defines it, a mindful leader is one who can influence others for better.

I had the good fortune of attending one of Janice Marturano's courses on being a mindful leader. The course looks to instill practices of mindfulness aimed specifically at a workplace audience. It ranges from amazing insights on how meditation can provide space for one to develop the qualities of a leader, to activities designed to help create more calmness and clarity in one's life.

I have taken this great wisdom that Janice presents and tried to put my own spin on it, framing it in the most tangible way for you. This chapter aims at increasing your capacity to influence for the better, to be a mindful leader. In order to do this, one needs to cultivate a natural capacity to have greater:

- Focus
- Clarity
- Creativity
- Compassion

First, Focus: this is the idea that one needs to stay attentive when necessary. You need to be present in the moment whether it be during an important business meeting or a small conversation with a coworker. It is important to focus on what is in front of us.

Second, Clarity: the ability to know how to react in the moment. Clarity is having a greater understanding of the current situation and being able to respond in a way that makes sense, and in a way that is for the betterment of those around you.

Third, Creativity: or to use a buzzword in 21st-century businesses, innovation. By cultivating a greater sense of spaciousness in our mind, we can start to put things together in new ways, increasing our ability to be creative.

Finally, Compassion: or in the context of this chapter, a deep understanding, and care for others. This is an extremely important thing in business and in life. People will often confide in those that they can trust. By simply listening to others and providing them compassion, one can have a profound impact.

The only catch with this and all of these traits is that you cannot do them in hopes of getting something for yourself. You have to truly care about another person, and not do it simply to be seen as a leader. But if you truly do care and you do put the effort into strengthening these characteristics of yourself, you can have a real impact.

## INCREASING FOCUS

Multi-tasking is a myth.

Sorry to burst your bubble, but it's true. Studies have proven that an excess of 30% of productivity is lost during multitasking and that employees are much less effective when they try to work on multiple things at once.[22]

Multi-tasking has become something that we have all adopted, thinking that we can work better while we are listening to music, watching TV, checking our Instagram feed, and so on. But really all of these things simply become distractions, and while there is a time and place for them, they are not helpful while working.

---

22 Mautz, S. 2017. "Psychology And Neuroscience Blow-Up The Myth Of Effective Multitasking". *Inc.*

You might be sitting there right now thinking that I am full of shit and that you are a rare exception who can handle multiple things at once. I am sure that you can. I am sure that you can watch TV and write an essay, but I promise you that you will be able to write a better essay and write it faster if you simply sat down and just focused on it.

In order to increase focus, it is important for us to learn how to give our full attention to one thing at a time, to be present in whatever task we are performing.

In order to help us do this, we are going to implement a technique called the "purposeful pause." I have borrowed this one from Janice's course. She talked about the importance of purposeful pauses or picking a specific activity throughout the day (i.e. drinking coffee, brushing your teeth…) to try to pay attention to the present moment, to take a pause from the busy-ness of the day and just be present. By paying attention to one action, no matter how big or small, we start to appreciate what it feels like to be present.

Purposeful Pauses:

- Think about your day, what is something that you do every single day of the week?
    - I chose a few: drinking coffee, walking into class (or a meeting), brushing my teeth.

- Once you have selected these, try to take a pause during these activities and truly immerse yourself in the present action as if you were doing it for the first time.
    - For example: often it can feel like an emotional drain to walk into a long class or a meeting feeling like your time could be better spent elsewhere. But do you remember what it felt like to walk into that first class of the semester or your first meeting at a new job? The eagerness and excitement that you felt before you started to settle into this routine or habit. Try to channel that feeling.
- When you approach the door to class or the meeting, take a minute to pause outside, just a quick second to try to place yourself in the present moment.
- This simple act of pausing can help stop the feeling of juggling so many things at once and can actually add a lot of purpose to whatever activity you are about to perform.When we can learn to be present in the little moments, we can start to expand this understanding to our greater work environment, allowing us to increase our overall focus. The hope is that these little moments start to become minutes, then hours and then days that we spend in the present, time that we spend focused dedicating our energy to the task at hand. It is with this focus, that we can be more efficient.

The next time you think about turning on the TV while you work, or watching a few YouTube videos before studying, try to pause for a second and sit in the moment. You may continue as planned, turning on the TV and that isn't a problem, but you have at least created the space to decide whether or not this is truly of benefit. Who knows, one day you might take that pause and decide otherwise.

## DEVELOPING CLARITY

A clear mind has the capacity to be a focused mind. A focused mind can be a present mind. A present mind **is** a happy mind.

Clarity and focus go hand and hand. While it is important to give something your full attention, if your mind is muddled, it will not have the space to absorb whatever is in front of you. It's like meeting someone for the first time and for some reason you cannot remember their name even though they said it a minute ago. It is because there is so much going on in your brain, that there simply was no room to learn anything new in that moment.

Clarity is not something that is easy to develop. It is not as though I can look at you and say, "Clear your mind" and you will respond "okay, done." Our minds are often filled with so many thoughts and feelings that it can feel extremely difficult to have any clarity.

It is very difficult to teach one how to develop more clarity, but there are exercises that can help create more order in one's life. This will help us to have a clearer understanding of our day and our week, allowing us to stay on top of our lives before our busy days overwhelm us.

When I think about clarity, I often think about organizing a messy room. Equating our minds to a messy bedroom, we can picture clothes all over the floor, an unmade bed, a disorganized desk, and so on. This mess is similar to the hundreds of thoughts that occur in our minds throughout the day. Now while we don't want to get rid of all of our thoughts, just like we don't want to just get rid of everything in our room, we would benefit from some greater organization. When everything is in its right place, we actually have the time and space to work on something new, to direct our focus where we want it, instead of being distracted by the mess.

I have personally dealt with this. There have been days where I go into work, or when I used to walk into the library to study and I would just sit there for a few minutes, maybe even a few hours and feel like I got nothing done. It can often feel like we are dedicating a lot of time to do the things we need to but for some reason, no progress is being made.

For me, the best way to attack this problem was to start writing "to-do" lists. Much like the motivations we set at the beginning of this book, a small, short to-do list can set an intention for how this work session needs to go. Just like the motivations, these can be long-term goals or simply short-term, more immediate tasks.

To-Do Lists:

- This practice is great for when you walk into work, or if you are heading to the library for a few hours of studying.
- Think about everything that you have to do and quickly scribble it all onto some scrap paper. By simply getting everything onto paper, it can help erode some of the overwhelming feelings associated with our busy schedules. Instead of having to remember everything in our heads, we can see it all right there in front of us.
- Look at this list and start to circle and mark the things that need to get done first. Also, if there is something big on the list, a task that might take a lot of work, try to write down some smaller objectives within the task.
  - example: my to-do list for the past few months has consisted of "Write a Book," but obviously I am not going to write a book in a day, so I would break up this task into smaller ones like "Write the chapter on Mindful Leadership."
- Write a new list, one that has some neatness and organization to it, where you have the tasks written in order of their importance.
- If you can, try to do the biggest, most important task first. Often we avoid this task because it is too daunting, but try to

accomplish this early, when you have the most drive, the most energy and I promise you will thank yourself in the long run.

- Optional: write a few smaller tasks, ones that would be very easy to achieve, such as "send an email to..." something that is easy to accomplish so that you can cross something off and feel like you are making progress. You can even make the first task: "write a to-do list." That is an easy one to cross off!

Once our rooms (our minds) have a little more organization, we will have the space to devote our focus to what is necessary. We will be able to sit and pay attention in class or during a meeting without thinking about all of the things we have to do.

Greater clarity comes from greater organization. When we are not trying to deal with a million different things at once, we have a better grasp of what is going on in the moment and are able to give all of our attention to the job at hand.

**✱✱**

A friend once asked me, "Andrew, I think this material is great, but I am already all about 'to-do' lists. Right now, I feel like they just get longer and longer. Is there anything else I can do to enhance my clarity?"

Beyond just pure organization, clarity also allows us the space to make rational decisions. To-do lists can help us create the conditions for clarity, but what do we do when we are thrust into a situation and our mind blanks on the answer? How do we handle a difficult question when our mind is so full of other thoughts? In high-pressure situations, like interviews or important meetings, this can and does happen.

I remember during one of my job interviews I was asked a question that placed me in a situation like this. I had been having some relationship troubles and my mind was anywhere but on the oil market. Spoiler alert, this is when my interviewer asked me, "How I thought oil prices would impact the private wealth management business?" My brain was scrambling to find the answer, but there was so much going on that I couldn't find anything. I got nervous and tried to come up with an answer, pulling complete garbage out of my ass claiming that the changes would affect the market and stock prices trying to use every buzzword I had in my repertoire.

It was in this example that I realized how uncomfortable I was with silence, feeling like I desperately needed to fill the space. But what if I did the opposite? What if I embraced the silence, and asked for a minute to gather my thoughts, allowing me to pause and return with a more succinct and clear answer? This idea can only help you. On one hand, if you actually know the answer, but your brain is too crowded with other thoughts, the pause can give you some space to think. On the other hand, if you can't come up with anything new, it probably means you don't know the answer and that is okay too, you aren't going to know everything, and neither is the person asking you the question. So next time something like this happens in a conversation with a friend or an important meeting, try to embrace the silence, use it is a time to gather your thoughts, to clear your head and remain focused on the task at hand.

To-do lists can help clear up your mind, but they aren't going to solve everything. Just because the tasks are now on paper, doesn't mean they go away. You don't have to accomplish them right away, just like in meditation, how you don't need to understand your thoughts immediately, rather you just recognize their existence and try to let them pass. But as it goes, these thoughts and the chaos of the brain will emerge again, and taking a pause to re-center yourself and gain some greater clarity can be a huge help.

## THE CREATIVE MIND

We are living in an age where in order to succeed in business innovation is required. However, many of us are so focused on innovation that we are unable to achieve it. Like trying

harder to meditate, trying and trying to think of a new innovation can be self-defeating. Rather than coming up with
novel and groundbreaking ideas, our minds are just looping
in circles unable to produce anything new.

Creativity comes when there is enough space for new ideas.
When your mind is calm, clear and focused, you allow associative networks to form in new and interesting ways. Think
about it like this, have you ever been asked a question and
the answer is on the tip of your tongue but for some reason
you just cannot remember it no matter how hard you try.
Then finally at the most random point, it finally comes to
you. Often this "ah-ha" moment can come at the weirdest
time, usually, the time when figuring out the answer is the
last thing on your mind. That is why the answer often comes
in the shower, or the middle of the night, or while driving,
times when our brains have space.

When our minds have a little space, when they are not so
occupied trying to figure out the answer and we can finally,
with ease, put together the associative networks to answer
that question we tried so hard to figure out.

This is where meditation can really be useful. A set, daily
practice can become the requisite for having a calm, clear,
and focused mind.

Another activity that I have found helpful in generating a more creative mind is to employ this part of your mind in lower stress situations. Personally, I am not a good artist, I cannot play any instruments, and I cannot sing to save my life. So, my creative side comes out in cooking. I try to test my brain by opening the fridge and trying to come up with new dishes that I could make. Although I know, I could mess up the meal and be forced to order pizza, it is fun to try and most of the times it turns out to be edible at worst. Not to brag but all this creative experimentation has made me a pretty good cook.

The point is that you need to flex your creative muscles so that when you actually have to employ them they are ready. It is like training for a marathon. You train and run day after day not just for the heck of it but so that you can eventually compete in and finish a marathon. By training your creative mind in low-stress situations, you create the conditions necessary to accomplish difficult tasks in high-pressure environments.

## BEING COMPASSIONATE

This is one of the most important traits that a leader must possess. Often when I think of people who have inspired my journey it is those who have shown me compassion. The people who have taken the time to listen to me, and help me on my path.

To me, this trait is required of a leader, especially a good one. Compassion, which I define here as a deep understanding and care for others, is a leader's ability to listen to the people he or she is influencing, to make people feel heard, respected, and important.

Compassion is also very hard to teach for it is nearly impossible for one to fake compassion. Therefore, in order to truly strengthen this side of yourself, you have to intrinsically desire to do so.

There are many meditation practices that I think are perfect for strengthening compassion. Some of which we have gone over like *loving-kindness* and *Tonglen*. Here I present another practice. One I think is extremely useful in life when dealing with others.

"I am just like you."

This is the name of a very powerful practice that requires you to put yourself in the shoes of a fellow employee or classmate (actually, the practice can be done with anyone, but for the sake of the exercise I am framing this toward a work or school environment). It is often helpful to start with a person with whom you feel comfortable, a co-worker or a classmate whom you consider to be a good friend. As you get more comfortable with this practice, you will progress forward, doing the same exercise for an employee that you struggle with, one who tends to push your buttons.

I am just like you:

- Start by taking some deep breaths trying to settle into a state that is both relaxed and alert.
- Call to mind the image of a co-worker or a classmate, one that you consider a close friend. Picture them sitting in front of you and try to hold their image in your mind.
- Now, place yourself within the other person's body, try to imagine that you are seeing the world from their eyes. Try to imagine how they feel. What do they struggle with, what makes them happy? Think about this for a few minutes.
- As you think about this try to see that, just like you, this person has challenges, they also struggle, and just like you, that person just wants to overcome this struggle and achieve happiness. In this sense, you are both very similar. Hold onto this notion; sit with it for a few moments.
- As you step back into your own mind, look at this person in front of you with the newfound knowledge that they are just like you, and you are just like them.
- As you would want done for you, wish them the accomplishment and achievement of all of their hopes and desires by whispering to the image in front of you: "May you have whatever is your heart's desire."

- Letting the image of that person fade, go back to the place of calm that you cultivated in the beginning.
- Now try to start this practice again with an individual whom you find to be difficult, cultivating this same feeling that this person is just like you. This version will be harder, but the more you do it the more similarities you will find between you and the person at hand. This will naturally allow you to feel a deeper connection to and compassion for this individual.

It is in this exercise that you can start to form feelings of kindness and compassion toward these people in your life, even the ones with whom you struggle. By stepping into someone else's shoes and seeing how deep down we are all so very similar, we can cut through some of the differences that have wedged a wall between us and other people. This practice helps us to tear down that wall rather than building it higher.

## BE A LEADER

Where are you now in your life, in your career?

It is easy to feel like we need a title in front of our name in order to be a leader. Often, we believe that as an analyst we are forced to just "do our time," putting in the work in order just to get somewhere else. To some extent this can be true. That first job out of college is usually the one where you just have to put in the long hours in order to do whatever the company needs. While on the surface our business card says analyst, we do not need to be reduced to just this title. We still have a purpose; we still have a reason to be here. Think back to the story of the janitor who wowed JFK.

No matter where we are on the totem pole, we have a purpose.

Anyone can be a leader. Anyone can influence for the betterment of others and maybe you already do. Whether you are a leader now or you are striving to become one, it is important to remember that you too can benefit from these practices. Wherever your journey takes you, be a leader: be focused, be clear, be creative, and be compassionate.

*"Your potential is endless, but your energy is not. Be patient and live for what matters most now. There's no doubt that you'll change the world, but it won't happen in a day's time."*

— FRIEND OF MIND, AGE 21

# CHAPTER 15

# THE SKEPTICAL GURU

—

*"Be curious, tap into that curiosity and know what curiosity feels like."*

— DR. JUDSON BREWER, DIRECTOR OF RESEARCH
AND INNOVATION AT THE MINDFULNESS
CENTER AT BROWN UNIVERSITY

It is totally okay to be skeptical of meditation. Naturally, it is a technique that seems a little too good to be true. It is a practice that has been shown to only affect your life in a positive way and it is completely free. This is where the average 21st-century consumer says, "Where's the catch?"

There is none.

Well, the only thing is that you need to open your mind; you need to go into the practice with a positive attitude. You can still be 100% skeptical but try to keep an open mind, try to think that the practice might work. You don't have to buy anything, you don't need to enter your credit card information, you just need to have a little bit of faith and then see for yourself.

Meditation was so appealing to me for these very reasons. Nobody was trying to sell me anything like a used car salesman, rather they just told me about the magic and beauty of this practice and if I felt so inclined, the door was wide open. No one was going to force me, and no one was going to be upset if I chose otherwise.

I want you to feel like I did when starting this practice. I want you to know that I will not be offended if you hate meditation, if all of these ideas sound crazy to you and you want nothing to do with them. It won't bother me because the only way meditation works is if you do it for yourself. It is not enough for me to want this for you; you need to want this for yourself.

So, if this practice is not for you that is fine. This practice is by no means for everyone at this moment, and at the very least, you know that meditation exists and have the opportunity to explore it when you are ready. But if there is any chance that this practice could impact you in some way, then keep reading and find out how to start building this practice, how to become a skeptical guru.

## TIME

Time: the most precious resource on the planet, the one thing that we can never get more of, something that has no monetary value but yet would be worth all the money in the world.

Time is something we all want more of – we will never have enough. In today's world, it can often feel like we are doing a million things all at once. Our days are an endless journey of struggling to get out of bed in the mornings and desperately climbing back into it at the end of the day. Not saying that this is every day, but we have all had moments where the first thing we think of when we get out of bed, is when we can get back into it.

My point is that people are busy. The little free time they do have is often spent doing other recommended activities like eating, sleeping, work, laundry, and exercising. People feel they simply do not have time for meditation.

"It sounds nice, but I just don't have the time right now" is by far the most common excuse I can think of. Frankly, it used to be the excuse I would use myself when I would skip a day of meditation, claiming that I was just too busy that day. It is always easy to say we are too busy. It is much harder to overcome this excuse in order to try something new, in order to step out of our comfort zone and see what the world has to offer.

**

5 minutes. I am going to go out on a limb and say that you have a free 5 minutes somewhere in your day. To give you some context, 5 minutes is practically the time you spend brushing your teeth morning and night and 99% of us manage to find the time, some of us even more than twice a day (also if you are in the 1% that doesn't, please start brushing your teeth).

Finding the time:

- Think about your entire day, from the moment you wake up to the minute you go to bed. Think about every activity you engage in.
- What are the things that you have to do like going to class (maybe) or going to work (definitely) or even going to the gym?
- Now think about all the things you choose to do. Maybe it's taking a long lunch, watching TV, scrolling through social media.
- See if you can find the time in this second category to make space for meditation. Maybe you spend a little less time

scrolling on social media; maybe you watch one less episode of Netflix; maybe you just try waking up 5 minutes earlier.

- All of us can find 5 minutes in our day, it is just about creating the motivation to do so, and I know you can do it.

If you really want to put this exercise to the test, document everything you do throughout an entire day in quarter hour increments. Write down what you did during these times and I promise that you will see gaps, places where you can actually find the time to sit.

## SPENDING TIME TO MAKE TIME

*"It is not about the years in your life, but the life in your years that counts."*

— ADLAI STEVENSON, AMERICAN LAWYER,

POLITICIAN, AND DIPLOMAT

Yes, we cannot change how fast time moves and we cannot make it stand still, but we can make each day feel more fulfilled and special. This is what meditation has done for me and so many other people.

Yes, it sounds crazy that in the hectic-ness of the 21st century that you could find time in your day to sit down and do absolutely nothing, but truly this practice allows you to keep moving in beat with the world's drum. Meditation can prevent burnouts, it can give you a nice feeling of resetting and being ready to get back to the world.

Meditation is not a time waster but a time saver. By taking a little bit of time every day to quiet your mind and go within yourself, you can spend the rest of the day doing the things that the world asks of you. Whether it be socializing, going to class, working a long day, going to the gym, all of these things can be aided with a solid foundation in your day, a practice that helps you center yourself and helps you feel ready to take on the world, a practice of meditation.

Meditation means being in the present moment, a practice that can provide tangible benefits in other aspects of your life. With this understanding, you can motivate yourself to sit for five minutes, and give this a try. And slowly, over time, you will start to become more present. While previously you might have studied while listening to music, and having your phone out, and watching TV, meditation can help you to let go of these distractions. Meditation can show you the beauty that lies in the present moment, allowing you to focus all of your efforts on what is in front of you right now. It may sound counter-intuitive, but meditation helps you save time. By giving a few minutes you could save hours.

## MINDFUL BREATH

One of my friends told me a story about the first time he interacted with meditation. He was out in Seattle and decided that he would go check out a Buddhist monastery. He had been hearing a lot about meditation and figured he'd see where all the buzz was coming from.

He walked into the door and instead of being given a how-to guide for practicing, he was placed in the back of the room to sit for 45 minutes as the monks went through their routine of chanting and meditating. I can tell you that 45 minutes is a long time, even for an experienced practitioner.

While it may sound cool to say that you just meditated with the monks, as a beginner, I doubt your parting thoughts will be "Wow, I need to start meditating." In fact, I imagine the feeling would be the opposite, thinking, "I'm going to leave meditation to the monks."

In my opinion, a crash course that throws you right into the fire without any warning or set up is not the way to start a practice. It would be like going to the gym for the first time and a trainer tells you to run a marathon on the treadmill.

If you have ever meditated before, you quickly learn that it is not easy to sit for 20 minutes straight. It's not easy to sit for even 5 minutes straight. It is strenuous on the back, your legs fall asleep, and not to mention your brain is moving at 1000 miles per hour.

So, in my experience, it is best to ease into this practice. To try to be honest with yourself about how much time you can commit every day, because it really is that daily commitment that leads to the big changes.

*"When building a practice, ask yourself... how much can I practice every day?"*

— DR. RICHARD DAVIDSON

This is the advice that Dr. Davidson gives to those who feel moved to start meditating. He recommends that you be realistic and think, "How much time can I actually devote to this practice?" If the answer is 30 seconds then Davidson says, try to do that every day, it is better than nothing.

Chade-Meng Tan in his book, *Search Inside Yourself,* discusses the concept of a mindful breath. A mindful breath is just as it sounds. The idea being that if you cannot get yourself to sit down for even 30 seconds that you should at least try and take one mindful breath every day.

The Mindful Breath

- Pick a point in your day where you will remember to do this.
- For me, I tend to use this practice every time I walk out of the door in the morning and step into the outside air.
- If you are doing the same as I, you will stop the second you walk outside and take a quick second to be present.
- Take a nice deep breath in and let it out until there is no air left in your lungs. Try to feel the entire breath enter and leave your body.
- Then go and have a great day.

This practice can help ground you, setting the tone for the day. When you can start your day from a place of calm, and centeredness, you can offer this wonderful sentiment outward to those around you. It is an excellent practice even for those who are avid meditators, for it is a simple reminder to be present. This is a practice that can be used at multiple points in the day and is great for resetting and replacing yourself in the moment.

So, if you really can't find any time to sit throughout the day, at least try this. Try and take one breath focusing all of your attention on the act.

## I DON'T NEED THIS

This practice helps people who are suffering; it fuels people who are happy; and, it provides a solid grounding for any human being.

In the scheme of things, our lives are so short; we are but a blip on a long timeline. And I am willing to bet that each one of us has had a day that went by so fast it was like we didn't even live it. Whether it is a full day's time spent hung-over in bed, or hours of binge-watching TV, we have all had days where it feels like we are not present.

Now if you are sitting here and saying that you love these days and your ideal day is spent watching TV and lying in bed, then I 100% respect that and I say you keep doing you. However, if you are anything like me, you might still spend the day in bed, but it will feel like something was missing, feeling like the day might have been wasted. It is that feeling when 11 a.m. becomes 5 p.m. in the blink of an eye and you are like "Where did today go?"

Meditation is not a cure-all practice, and thus far it may seem like I am preaching it as such, but in no way does meditation fix all of life's ups and downs. It certainly has not eradicated my occasional weekend day of binge-watching TV and incessant snacking. It has however, provided me an anchor, a strong foundation

I can turn to when it feels like my days are starting to slip away from me.

If you feel like you don't need this practice, I just ask that you think about this question:

*Is there anywhere in my life where I would like to be more present?*

If the answer is yes, I think it might be worthwhile to see if getting your butt on the cushion can provide something for you.


## RELIGION

Meditation is not a religion; it is a practice.

Often people worry that meditation will conflict with their religious beliefs that meditation will force them to convert to another faith. However, quite the opposite is true. Meditation can make you a better practitioner of your faith and has for many individuals.

I myself was born Jewish, went to a Quaker high school, a Catholic, Jesuit University, and have a very strong affinity toward Buddhism at this point in my life. Meditation has not caused me to abandon my religion. Rather meditation has allowed me to enjoy the lessons I have learned from each faith. I think back to the practices of the Jewish Sabbath and try to invoke some of these ideals, like stepping away from technology for the day. I reminisce on my days of Quaker Meeting, finding the silence I observed there to be a basis for my practice. I strongly believe in the principles of my Jesuit education and caring for the entire person. And most recently, I have cultivated a huge interest in the principles of impermanence that Buddhism presents.

Meditation has not torn me away from any of these but has rather allowed me to see them in a new light. I have found a new appreciation for the plethora of traditions I have been exposed to and have allowed them to shape me into the person I am today, accepting all that they have to offer.

You too can find the same. Regardless of what your religion is, you can benefit from being more present. This newfound present-ness can actually make you a better observer of your faith as you can give more of yourself to the traditions and prayers.

The more research I did, the more shocked I was by the presence of meditation in various religions. In Catholicism, the silence of meditation allows you to form a deeper connection with God. In the Quaker tradition, it is believed that in the silence, God will speak to the light inside of each of us, empowering us to speak our message. In Judaism, meditation allowed for contemplation of key elements of the religion, allowing you to form a deeper and more personal understanding of the message.

Meditation does not need to conflict with whatever your beliefs are, rather it can augment them, allowing you to understand on a more personal level.

## THE OLE COLLEGE TRY

I remember first understanding this phrase in the weeks leading up to college, thinking about how I could redefine myself in a new environment. I realized that college is the perfect time to try new things. It is the perfect place to pick up new hobbies like rock climbing or possibly even meditation.

I am sure almost everyone has heard this phrase. The ole college try indicates that you are in a time in your life where you have an ample amount of free time, a plethora of activities available to you and tons of people to do them with you. College is a time where trying things is not only possible but also recommended.

This is the same attitude I want you to have with meditation. Whether you are in college right now or haven't even thought of a classroom in years, it is never too late to try something new.

The best part of the idiom is that it implies this sense of open-mindedness, this willingness to try something not because someone is forcing you to but because you are curious, truly curious thinking that you may enjoy it.

So, this is my request of you. If you are skeptical of meditation and are thinking right now that I do not want this practice, I do not need this practice, then at least give it a try. Even if you only do it one time, at least you tried. Even if you do it for only 30 seconds, at least you put the effort in. Who knows, it could be something you never think about again or it could become something you do every day for the rest of your life.

\*\*

Ultimately, meditation is not something that can be forced. You need to decide that it is right for you in this moment. You can keep reading this book, you can keep studying the science, you can hear hundreds of success stories, but you won't figure it out until you see for yourself.

It is like reading a book about fitness. Just reading the book isn't going to get you toned abs, but actually implementing the things you have learned, that will make a difference.

*"Remember the best experiences come from going outside of your comfort zone. That it's okay if things aren't amazing to start, the point is to be uncomfortable, but to do all of these things anyway and reap the benefits of the experience. It usually turns out great."*

— FRIEND OF MIND, AGE 22

# CHAPTER 16

# STRUGGLING MINDFULLY

———

"You really are enough, it may not feel that way but you, just as you are, are enough and you are whole and loved and you need to find the way back to that essential truth."

— YAEL SHY, AUTHOR OF *WHAT NOW: MEDITATION FOR YOUR TWENTIES AND BEYOND*

Meditation can sometimes be just what the doctor ordered. When we are feeling down or overwhelmed, or even worse than that, feeling depressed and hopeless, meditation can be the perfect medicine.

Meditation is an insight practice and as we discussed earlier in the book, it can be extremely useful at showing what is going on within us at this moment. We are then able to get more comfortable with these feelings, and then naturally they start to hold less power over us. Finally, we learn to overcome them.

Give you an example?

Well, I am glad you asked. For most of my life, every emotion that I experienced was expressed as anger. If I was sad, I would get angry. If I was scared, I would get angry. And when I was angry of course I would get angry. Anger out of the emotions in my emotional arsenal was the easiest to for me to understand. So, when my emotions started to overwhelm me, anger was the only thing that made sense. Meditation allowed me to gain a greater comfortability with my own insecurities and fears. It has helped me to comprehend deep emotional states, allowing me to understand what I am truly feeling. So now instead of just being angry, I can notice if I am actually just sad. When I know what I am feeling, it is then much easier to give myself the love and attention I need.

It is a very common occurrence for a person to have an outlet for strong emotion. Jeff Roth, a meditation teacher, used to associate every emotion with hunger, which unless you have a good metabolism is a very difficult burden to bear.

Emotions can be tricky and can often cause us to shut down and to act in ways contrary to who we are and who we want to be. However, if we can find the root of those emotions, find out what is really driving our reaction we might be able to make a huge change in our lives.

Instead of allowing these emotions to overwhelm you and cause you to act without focus and clarity, what if we could see what was going on below the surface? What if we could realize that the anger was actually deep sadness? It is realizations like this that allow us to start solving our own problems.

**

I tend to eat when I am anxious. For example, during the writing process of this book, I was so worried that I would never finish that rather than sit down and write I just kept walking around my kitchen trying to find a snack. I would take a bite of chocolate, but not be satisfied. I would go for some chips and think it was just what I wanted, so I would have a few more until I got bored with those, at which point I would reach for the chocolate again.

Shortly after my snacking rampage, I realized that I wasn't even hungry to begin with. In reality, I had just eaten a nice filling dinner and the desire to snack was not out of hunger, rather it was to fill a hole that I was ignoring.

It wasn't until I sat down at the desk that I had gotten to know very well over the past few weeks that I realized I had no desire to turn on the computer. I had absolutely no desire to write any words.

"Was I eating in order to avoid writing?"

As I thought about this, I realized that there was more going on here… I started to explore what was behind my aversion to writing. I started coming up with ideas in my head checking them to see if they felt right—you know when you explain a feeling and you just can feel in your gut, in your bones that you hit the nail on the head; that was what I was looking for.

"I am eating in order to avoid writing, I am avoiding writing because I am worried that the book will turn out poorly and therefore putting more effort into it is futile. I am eating because I feel like I am not good enough, like I am not worthy of writing this book. I am eating because I feel inadequate."

This was it. This is what I was feeling, this deeper feeling was causing an action that I did not want to occur. My relationship with this book and further, my relationship with myself, were causing me to eat.

Now the goal is to stop it before it happens.

Two minutes ago, I had the same feeling. As I started to write this section, I immediately felt hungry. Trying to avoid it, I kept writing, but, a minute later I found myself standing up from the chair and making my way to the kitchen as if someone else was driving my body.

Thinking about this chapter, the words and lessons I am trying to portray to you I stopped and thought "am I really hungry? Or am I just trying to avoid writing again? Am I just worried that this book is no good?"

I didn't grab any snacks and I returned to my chair to continue typing the words that you are reading. This is the power of mindfulness in action. It allows us to see what is going on within us at this very moment. Even though this example is a small victory, it shows me the power I have to control my actions. It allowed me to realize that I wasn't actually hungry but rather trying to avoid another feeling, a much deeper one. You too can do the same.

## RAIN

Rain is analogous to our emotions. Some days it can pour, others it drizzles, but regardless, there is often a beautiful rainbow after a monstrous storm.

RAIN is a practice that borders the fence between meditation and self-reflection. RAIN is meant for dealing with strong emotions and trying to help yourself through them. This four-step practice is one that can provide incredible self-insight.

R – Recognize

A – Accept

I – Inquire

N – Non-Identification (or preferably Nourish)

**\*\***

As we have stated, meditation is a flashlight that shines on the dark corners of your mind.

Meditation will reveal things that you are trying to avoid. It is just natural. When the brain finally slows down and stops receiving the constant inputs that we provide it, it freaks out a little bit. Often one of two things happen. One is we fall asleep as that is usually the association the brain has with low activity. Or on the other hand, all of the things that we have been ignoring – the emotions, the feelings, and more that we have pushed away and replaced with distract-ing stimuli – can emerge when the brain has nothing to distract it. This can often be off-putting and can lead you away from the pillow.

This happened to me in the beginning of my practice. I would meditate for a few times, and I would think that it was the best thing in the world and then one day my brain started to have what I call pop-ups.

Imagine you are watching a hilarious video on your computer and all of a sudden, a way too accurate pop-up flashes onto the screen. Now I am not talking about an advertisement for something you thought about buying earlier in the day, that is creepy, and computers are becoming way too smart but that is not my point. I am picturing an incredibly detailed calendar notification that reminds you "Hey you have the biggest exam of your life tomorrow!" or "Hey you should really consider changing your eating habits!" A pop-up that reminds you about everything you have been avoiding.

That is never a good feeling, and it can often be incredibly defeating. For instead of shutting down the computer and doing what is required, it is easy to just keep going, to keep watching until we have really dug a deep hole for ourselves.

As you can imagine, when this state starts to emerge in meditation it can be very easy to throw in the towel, to say that meditation is causing me way too many problems.

The truth, those problems are there to begin with, meditation is just bringing them to the surface.

When these feelings arise, we need a tool to help overcome them. RAIN is that tool.

**

I remember the first time that I utilized this practice. It was a brisk Thursday morning in March, and I was on the phone with my mentor Rick. Rick had been helping me with my meditation practice for some time now.

On this particular morning, I remember not looking forward to his call. My meditation practice had not been going well, I had been struggling to remain present, and finding it difficult to convince myself to sit. So, when I saw his name appear on my phone, I immediately started thinking of excuses. "Hey Rick, sorry something came up," "Hey Rick, I forgot to study for a test," "Hey Rick, I am late for a shift at work." I didn't want to lie to someone who was helping me, so I figured I would tell him the truth.

I picked up the phone to hear the warm, welcoming voice of my mentor. Before he even had a chance to ask a question, I simply outlined what I was feeling. "Hey Rick, I really don't feel like talking today, I have been having a lot of trouble meditating and I think I just need to take some time away from it."

"Okay, not a problem," he said. There was a unique softness in his voice, almost as if he knew the exact position I was in. He followed up with, "Well there is a practice that might actually be helpful, it isn't really a meditation, but it might help."

I was reluctant, but how could I go on teaching meditation to my friends if I wasn't doing it myself? I figured anything was worth a try.

It was at this point that Rick referred to the practice of RAIN. Half-unsure what I was about to experience and half certain that he was going to just play rain noises on his phone while I listened and tried to relax, I took a seat on my cushion and awaited further instruction.

"So, you are dealing with some difficult feelings," he said, "Well, the first step in the process is to **recognize** what is going on." He told me to sit and look within, see if I could find any feelings or sensations in my body.

"I feel this electricity in my hands, like this desire to just let out pent-up energy."

"Is this where it starts?" he questioned.

"No, the energy just gathers in my hands." Ready to strike, I realized that my boxing days had left some lasting habits, "But the source is much deeper, I can feel it go all the way to my heart, like a tightness on the left side of my chest, almost as if someone is inflating a balloon inside of me."

I was still unclear how this was going to help me. I started to just feel angrier like the balloon in my chest was going to pop and I was going to yell at my mentor.

He told me to put my hands on the area of tightness and just sit for a few minutes with the feelings to see if I could **accept** they were there, noticing if the acceptance could cause the feeling in my chest to loosen.

"Is the feeling moving or changing?" breaking the silence he inquired as to what my progress was.

"A little bit, but not really. I still feel like my chest is going to explode".

"That is okay," he said, "you just need to accept that."

"Now I want you to **inquire** as to what may be going on at this very moment. Where do you think the tightness comes from? Take your time."

I sat and tried to come up with an answer, worrying that I would disappoint my mentor if I came up empty-handed. The more I thought about it, the less I could understand, the further I would drift from the problem at hand and be lost in thought somewhere else. So instead of trying to answer, I simply asked in my head, "What am I feeling right now?" Then I sat and waited for a response.

A few minutes went by and still nothing, but rather than give up, I continued to sit, confident that my intuition would provide the answer, that my mind would put together its associative networks and form an explanation.

Finally it did, and I was able to break the silence.

"I am worried that I am not good enough at meditation, that I have not practiced enough to be teaching other people, to be writing a book. How am I supposed to be the 'meditation guy,' if I cannot even focus during the practice myself?"

This was it.

I knew this was the right answer. I could feel the tension in my chest start to evaporate. I felt extremely emotional, I couldn't tell if I was going to cry, scream, breakdown, or smile. It was as if I had dislodged a ginormous rock that had been blocking my emotions from being felt and understood.

"Now that you know what you are dealing with, see if you can **nourish** yourself. Give yourself the love and understanding that a mother would give to her newborn baby. It is okay to not be a perfect meditator, you are where and who you are, and that person is more than enough."

Listening to these wise words from my mentor, I started to nourish myself, silently telling myself that it was okay not to be perfect. I didn't need to be the best meditator in the world. I just needed to be me and stop worrying about trying to be better than who I am and where I am right now.

R – Recognize

A – Accept

I – Inquire

N – Nourish

## COMPARING MIND

(S)he is so much better than I am.

We have all been here, frankly, we can't help it. We constantly compare ourselves to others. Whether it be a co-worker, a friend, a famous person or even some random stranger on the street. We tend to have this mindset of comparing our performance, our actions, our bodies, ourselves to others.

This problem has started to become much worse in the last few decades – with the invention of the internet and the speed and methods with which we can disseminate information, much of which is slanted or false. This also means we have access to more people. Previously, your comparisons would only be made to close friends and family. Now, people are comparing their bodies to models, their career trajectory to billionaires, and their lives to those whom they don't even know but still deem to be better.

It has gotten even worse in the last few years. The emergence of social media allows the average person to post ideal snippets of their life. They can choose to show only the incredible and amazing parts, the parts that they would want to show the world. So now on top of the rich and famous, we find ourselves making comparisons to people who seem to have better lives than we do. We see their Instagrams and think they are better looking. We watch their Snapchats and think they have more friends and more fun.

Funny how we never compare down, we rarely think of how fortunate we are compared to others, more often we worry about how we stack up to those "better" than us.

This is what I refer to as the comparing mind: a mental process in which we make ourselves seem less compared to others.

**

I want you to think of a time where you compared yourself to another individual. Now I want you to walk through the process and see if at any point in this interaction the other person intentionally made you feel bad. Or rather did you do that to yourself?

One of the first instances that come to mind for me is comparing my body to others. In the current times, this seems to be a lot more prevalent. With magazines detailing the perfect physique, people posting their bodies on Instagram, and the world in a fitness craze, it can seem like we are never in the shape that we should be.

This is one of the easiest things to compare because it is all around us and it is very physical. Because of this you can put a picture of you next to a model and say that you do not look good enough. And with Instagram, you now see the perfect snapshots of other people's lives – people posing taking the perfect pictures, with the best angles in order to highlight their figure and physique. As my dad says, you can take a really bad picture of yourself shortly after an eating contest. Or you can fast for a few days, put on a little tanning lotion, get a high definition camera and post some great looking pictures, not to mention the amazing power of Photoshop and other apps that allow us to touch up the things we dislike. We are now comparing ourselves to what is often a false reality, thinking that people always look like they do in the things they post. It is this constant comparison that can erode our self-worth. Feeling like we need to look "better" be something other than who we are can be very self-defeating.

For me, this was an all too real occurrence, one that would cause me to reject meals with friends, workout until I could barely stand up, and put all of my efforts into the goal of looking like someone else.

I so desperately wanted to look like someone else, that I stopped being me. I was driven so much by the way I looked that I didn't want to go out until my physique had changed. In the summers throughout high school, I would always tell myself I would finally get the body I had been striving for, that way when I came back to school, people would be surprised and shocked and finally pay attention to me. The reality of it is that when I was really in shape, I didn't get any accolades, my life didn't change for the better, and I didn't even appreciate the effort I had put in!

The more I compared, the further down the rabbit hole I went. Even when my body started to change and mold with a layer of new muscle, I still felt like I needed to do more. I was always able to find people more fit than I, feeling like I always came up short. I needed to be bigger, more muscular, but yet not too big. I started digging in on specific parts of my body too. Thinking I needed a more defined chest, bigger biceps, toned abs. I started to literally pick myself apart, constantly feeling like I wasn't good enough.

**

The comparing mind is not something we can easily rid ourselves. Much like thoughts arising during a meditation, the comparing mind will arise naturally. You will walk by someone and think that they are better dressed than you, better looking, maybe even smarter. You might even start to put yourself down, saying that you need to buy better clothes, workout more, and read more books.

The comparing mind can really start to take hold of our actions, our mental processes, making us constantly feel less than we are.

How do we overcome this? How do we overcome the power of our own mind?

The answer: meditation.

Just as you recognize your thoughts and return to your breath, you will recognize when you are comparing and try to return to reality. As you start to do this repeatedly, you will slowly start to catch yourself, stopping yourself from making these comparisons before they occur.

If it is hard to return to reality, if you simply cannot get out of this mode of thinking, then heed the advice Yael would have given to herself: "You are perfect just the way you are." While it will be hard to feel this way at all times, this reminder might help show you that you do not have to be more than who you are right now. Even if you want to be somewhere else, to be better, just remember that this moment is a necessary grain of sand in a beautiful sandcastle – without it, the whole thing would come crashing down.

**

How did I overcome the difficulty surrounding my physique? How did I overcome my doubt, feeling like I was never good enough? How did I learn to manage my emotions?

Honestly, I haven't. These are all things that I deal with on a constant basis. Sometimes they overpower me, and I find myself deep in self-judgment, or self-doubt, or unable to express my emotions properly. But more often than not, I am able to prevent these feelings. I am able to recognize when I am comparing myself to others and see that my body, just like me, is unique and different. I am able to understand my doubt and remind myself that I am a hard worker and worthy of the things for which I strive. I am able to feel my emotions overwhelming me and take a step back, assessing what is truly going on here and acting from a place of insight.

In order to be happy, in order to love myself, I just need to be me — even if this means dealing with judgment, doubt, sadness, and anger. All of these things are part of me and rather than ignore them, I can embrace them, understand them and use them to my betterment. We can still make changes, still work hard and still have desires and emotions, but they should not be driven by other forces. Our feelings and wants should be within our comprehension, for with insight comes power.

*"It's sometimes scary to think that you are the only one that can truly make you happy, but once you embrace that principle, you will live a truly happy and peaceful life."*

—FRIEND OF MIND, AGE 18

CHAPTER 17

# AVERAGE JOE, TURNED MEDITATION EXPERT

———

*"Good Luck, Bad Luck, Who Knows..."*

— CORY MUSCARA, MINDFULNESS

SPEAKER, COACH AND TEACHER

We have immediate, almost reflexive judgments about our daily interactions, categorizing an exchange or event as good, bad, or neutral. It has become such a habit that we often find even in meditation, a place reserved for no judgment, we start to criticize ourselves, beating ourselves up when we realize we are lost in thought. However, is this really a negative experience? Frankly, no, this is the most powerful moment of meditation, the recognition that we are thinking; for now, we are capable of returning to our anchor, returning to the practice. As we do this over and over again, we go deeper and deeper into the practice and into ourselves, strengthening our ability to let thoughts pass rather than get continuously distracted by them. So really noticing we are thinking is a good moment in meditation not a bad one.

Cory Muscara, a meditation teacher, working to institutionalize meditation in healthcare and school settings reminded me of an excellent story with his quote above.

**

There was once a farmer in northern Europe who had a small plot of land with his son, some cattle, and a horse for transport. One day the horse ran away, his only way to travel between his house and the town some ten miles away.

When the townspeople heard, their hearts reached out saying, "What bad luck, how unfortunate."

The farmer surrendering to the way of the world simply responded, "Good luck, bad luck, who knows."

The next day, the horse came back with a pack of 10 wild horses, increasing the man's wealth and ability to travel.

The townspeople came back a resounding proclamation of good luck. "What good fortune" they told the man to which he responded the same, "Good luck, bad luck, who knows."

A few days later the farmer's son was trying to tame the horses, when one bucked, launching the boy in the air resulting in a broken leg.

Again, the townspeople aired their sorrows, telling the farmer, "What bad luck" and wishing the boy a quick recovery.

As you may imagine, the man responded with, "Good luck, bad luck, who knows."

The next day, the military came to recruit soldiers for the impending conflict, requesting all able-bodied young men. Seeing the boy's broken leg, they let him off allowing him to remain safe at home with his father.

**

It is impossible to know what will come of any event. We can go on and on, expanding this story to show that the same life experience can be viewed as both good or bad – lucky or unlucky, and ultimately, well beyond our control. We might think something is so incredibly unlucky, but that event may just be setting us up to reap some other reward. Like the old farmer says, "Who knows?"

So when you look at your life, your fate, your (mis)fortune, simply give in, try and accept whatever comes your way. Everything you have been through has gotten you to this exact moment, to this exact page, of this exact book, to the desire to learn more about yourself. That is, in my opinion, a great place to be.

## TEACHING YOUR FRIENDS

Become a teacher.

The best way to learn something inside and out is to teach it to someone else. This was something we all learned in school, the idea that you really know something when you can explain it in your own words to another person. Well meditation is no exception. When you can start sharing this practice with other people, it really takes on a special place in your heart.

This desire to teach/share helped me solidify my daily practice. One day I decided that I wanted to teach this to my friends because of how impactful it had been on my life. However, I had not yet established a daily practice of my own and I had an odd feeling about preaching what

I could not do myself. I was reminded of a story of about Mahatma Gandhi.

**

A woman brought her son to see Gandhi. She requested that Gandhi instruct her son to stop eating sweets.

"Gandhi, my son consumes far too much sugar, will you please tell him it's bad for his health?" the mother asked.

Gandhi listened to her request but did not give the boy any advice, instead, he told the boy and his mother to return in two weeks. They listened to his instructions, though unsure of his intention.

Two weeks later, the mother and son pair returned.

"Boy, you should stop eating sugar. It is not good for your health," Gandhi said without haste.

Confused, the mother questioned why Gandhi could not have just said this earlier, why did they have to leave and return two weeks later?

"Two weeks ago, I had an obsession with sugar. I needed that time to cut back myself," Gandhi said as he smiled back at them.

**

Being a good teacher requires that you practice what you preach. I mean imagine if your physics teacher didn't believe in Newton's first law of motion? That would first be crazy and second it would be very hard for you to believe anything he was teaching.

A good teacher cares about the subject material. You can see the passion in their eyes, their desire to be there. This is the teacher you want to become.

So, if you are intrigued by meditation and want to establish a daily practice and integrate the art deeper into your life, I recommend that you try to teach what you have learned to at least one person. It can be a parent a best friend, or even a stranger you meet on the bus. See if you can tell them about the beauty of meditation and how it has impacted and helped you.

This is an exercise for YOU! It does not matter whether this person starts meditating or not, but it will allow you to experience two things. One you laid the foundation for this person to start exploring meditation, and that is a true gift to give. Two, you have just learned more about your own practice, you have just reaffirmed your desire to meditate and you have strengthened your connection to the art. By explaining something in your own words, by putting your own spin on it, it becomes not just meditation, but YOUR meditation

So, go out and teach one person, or go crazy like me and try to teach every person you meet. I promise the strange looks don't seem as weird after you have explained meditation a few hundred times!

## CREATE A SANGHA

The air is different in a meditation community or sangha.

Anyone who has started meditating in a solitary environment can tell you the vast difference they can feel in a room full of meditators.

I remember the first time that I sat in on a large group meditation. Mid-way through the 30-minute session, I had to open my eyes just to remind myself that I wasn't in a trance. I felt as if everything had faded and I was totally at peace.

If you have no idea what I am talking about, do not worry, you will one day. There is a sense of security and support that comes from a sangha. Although meditation is an individual journey, having other people there reminds you of how connected we all are.

It is easy to get lost on this journey, to think that it is best to remove yourself from society and strive to achieve some greater mental state on your own. However, that is not our goal. We are more similar to others than we care to admit. We all suffer and we all want to be happy and meditation is an excellent way to help someone reach that goal. We should want to be present in this world, not to escape from it.

Support of a meditation practice is an incredible feeling. When you have a group of people who want to meditate with you, who want to share this experience with you, there is an energy that is indescribable.

\*\*

One of the greatest things college taught me is that if there is not a club or activity that you like, start your own.

Often times, meditation Sanghas are not easily accessible. Sometimes, it can be scary to go join a brand-new group. It might even feel as if there are no people similar to you who are partaking in this practice.

So, let's think back to this lesson that college teaches all of us. That we can all create the things that we want, we just have to be willing to take a leap and give it a shot, "the old college try". Whether it is just you and a friend, or a much larger group, meditation benefits from community and your practice will too.

## GOING ON A RETREAT

Learning meditation is a lot like learning a language. Anyone who has learned a second language can tell you that the classroom practice was helpful, but when you live in a country that spoke the language, when you speak it every day, that is when you really became fluent.

The same can be said for meditation, you can practice for a few minutes every day, but the real changes come from total immersion, when there is nothing else on your schedule, on your mind, then meditation. Think about it. If you went to a monastery and the teacher requested that you meditate for two hours without moving a muscle. One of two things will happen. One, you might say this is crazy and throw in the towel at some point, or two you might give it a go, struggle, but eventually, you break through that wall of resistance and when the two hours is up you will be shocked that you were able to do it. Yes, this may sound crazy now, but one day you might see it is actually quite normal.

When you are practicing meditation, you are often doing it with the intention of going on with your day afterward. So, while you might devote 20 minutes in the morning to the practice, this time will end, and you will be immediately reminded of the other items on your mental checklist. You might even be reminded of these obligations during your meditation. Often this mindset can even distract us as begin thinking about what comes next.

I have had times where I will be doing a morning sit and my brain will start racing as it often does. It will remind me of all the things that I have to do at work today, and all of the things that are on my calendar. It really starts to interfere with my meditation and before I know it, the bell has rung, and it is time for me to actually go and do all of these things.

A retreat environment is completely different. From what people have told me, mixed with my own personal experience, I can say with confidence that a daily practice is inches compared to the miles that can be achieved during a retreat.

Meditation retreats are just as they indicate, they are a time and space that is focused on meditation. They all have their own flavor and curriculum, but the premise is the same, it is a time for meditation and personal insight.

One of the retreats that I attended was through the Insight Meditation Community of Washington. It was a weekend long silent meditation retreat. Now I know how fun and exciting a weekend sitting in silence sounds, but I promise it really is a life changing experience and if you are interested in meditation I highly recommend giving it a try.

\*\*

As I pulled up to the retreat center I thought I must have been crazy. I had just recently started meditating and now I was going to spend an entire weekend sitting. If that wasn't crazy enough, I was going to have to remain silent as well.

It was early in the evening as I got out of the car and went to check in at the front desk. I was worried that I was going to have to interact without using my words. I thought about showing them my ID, so they could see my name without my having to say it. Luckily, a smiling face greeted me, and I was given permission to use my voice. This was the first and last time that I would speak for the entirety of the retreat.

After a few rule setting sessions and an evening meditation it was time for bed. 9:00 p.m., these people must have been crazy, I hadn't gone to bed that early since I was a baby. I tried to participate and partake in everything the retreat had to offer. I remember climbing into bed in a room with two roommates, both of whom I had not spoken a single word to. As I sat in bed trying to force the familiar feeling of sleep to overtake me, I remember feeling a sense of contentment, as if I was right where I needed to be. For the first time in a while, I was fully present. The darkness of sleep washed over me causing these thoughts to fade from my mind.

I awoke early in the morning in order to embark on a 13-hour journey of meditation. Excited to truly get into the practice, I eagerly awaited our 6:00 a.m. morning session. But after about 15 minutes, I was met with great resistance. My back started to hurt, my stomach started to rumble, I couldn't stop thinking about how much time had gone by.

"Oh no," I thought to myself.

If I was met with this much resistance within the first 15 minutes, how was I going to survive an entire day of just this?

Finally, the bell rang which meant we would transition to walking meditation. I was relieved and excited figuring a change would be perfect. I bundled up and walked out into a cold April Saturday for my first-ever walking meditation. Things were going well but after a few minutes, I was again met with resistance. The time just felt like it was moving in slow motion, it was driving me crazy.

This pattern went on and off as we started to cycle through walking, sitting, and eating all while trying to be mindful. Try as I might to get with the program, my resistance to the retreat would not fade.

**

Retreats aren't easy. They can be challenging and actually extremely difficult. They can test your ability as a meditator and a person, but that is what they are for. They are supposed to throw you right into the deep end so that you can quickly learn how to swim.

Like going to a new country to implement the language skills you learned in the classroom, it will be extremely difficult and strange at first. When you try to speak the new language, you might meet some resistance as your brain continues to operate in your native tongue, but little by little, you get used to it, you start to get comfortable. At some point, you have a huge breakthrough a time when you are speaking comfortably, and you don't even realize your dialect has changed.

Just like when you learn to ride a bike and it isn't until you look back to see no one holding you that you realize you can do it. It just feels natural.

**

I felt a cool breeze on the back of my neck. I was exploring a new part of the 7-acre property; I wanted to find a new location for my afternoon walking meditation.

At this point, I was exhausted. I had fallen asleep during the last meditation as I chose the laying down posture to ease the tension on my back. Not a great decision, but I just couldn't sit straight any longer.

As I tried to shake off the grogginess of my nap, I started to pay attention to my surroundings. I started to implement the practice of walking meditation. Focusing on my breathing I started to take some steps, one foot at a time. Breathing in, I lifted my foot off the ground, exhaling out I let it drop in front of me.

As I got deeper into the practice, my awareness started to expand beyond my breath. I could feel the connection in my whole body, from my brain to my breath to my feet keeping my entire being in motion, keeping me on track with the practice. I felt my connection with the outside world. I could hear the sounds of birds and the rustling of animals nearby.

All of a sudden, I stopped. I stood still as the voice in my head revealed wisdom that had been accumulated over the weekend. Things that I had subconsciously learned but had not yet put together.

*If animals can be content with just sleeping, sitting, eating, and walking, you can too.*

I thought about this idea. I started to contemplate why it was that humans were the only creatures that needed more, that wanted a good career, a nice home, and a good reputation. I started to question why we as humans wanted more than any other species we have discovered.

As I tossed this idea around my brain, I came to this conclusion: human beings have the gift of wanting more. We are blessed with a cognitive ability to strive for more than just survival. However, deep down we are basic animals and we too can benefit from these basic activities. We need to become comfortable with these activities in order to transcend beyond them and into our daily routines.

I was uncomfortable on this retreat because I felt like I should've been doing more with my time. It wasn't until I realized that this is exactly where I needed to be that I could truly be present.

**

The big difference about retreats is the ability to remove oneself from the busy-ness of everyday life. There are no calendars or meetings that you need to prepare for, rather there is a simple schedule of meditation, eating and sleeping.

My resistance to the retreat didn't dissipate entirely, but it did start to lessen, and I started to embrace the practice more. I was even disappointed to leave, finding true beauty and peace in just being rather than needing to do more.

Most of us cannot step away from our lives and spend the remainder of them in retreat. Luckily, we don't have to. There are many weekend or week-long retreats that can give us a reminder of what is the real meaning of our existence, allowing us to enjoy a simple way of life. With this knowledge, you can make the most out of the life that you are living. When you are content just meditating all day, imagine what you can do with all the tasks that are on your plate. As I often say, when you can enjoy sitting and simply focusing on the breath, you can get excited about doing practically anything.

Meditation, as we have defined it in this book, is a tool to place oneself in the present moment. Well a retreat provides the perfect conditions for being present.

**

As you build this practice, you begin to realize that life is short, much too short to spend the majority of it reminiscing on the past and planning for the future. This is why we need to live in the present. Why we need to make a conscious effort to live in each moment, trying to find meaning in everything life has to offer, the good and the bad.

I have begun to adopt my meditation practice into everything I do. Whether it is the way I think, the way I interact, the way I feel, I try to make meditation my life's work. It is such a powerful tool, and one that has really made a huge difference for me. Whether you are just starting, or an expert already, meditation has so much to show you about yourself and about the world. So keep building, keep learning, and remember, the present moment is yours as long as you:

*"Take everything in life one step at a time."*

— FRIEND OF MIND, AGE 21

# CHAPTER 18

# THINK BIGGER

———

*"Don't compare someone's middle to your beginning."*

— FRIEND OF MIND, AGE 21

This book contains more than just meditation. It is a story about happiness, about betterment, about life, about you and me and all of us.

What do you want to do with this knowledge?

Meditation is an incredible practice, it deserves continuous time and cultivation, and frankly I don't ever see myself stopping. I think that meditation is a lifetime art, a practice that one can always benefit from.

However, I do think that we can go beyond just the practice. We need to think bigger. Meditation allows us to help ourselves, to gain deeper insight, to spend more time in the present. But can we do something with all of these this knowledge?

In certain sects of Buddhism there is a being called a Bodhisattva. Without going into detail about the religions etymology, Bodhisattva's are beings that have achieved enlightenment and have broken out of the wheel of suffering but decide to continue to suffer in order to help others.

Think about it like this. A Bodhisattva is like a friend who already completed the marathon, but runs back to help you finish, choosing to run the extra distance by your side. The idea of a Bodhisattva is a beautiful one, it reminds me that we are not doing this practice for selfish reasons that we are not meditating just to leverage all of the benefits that accompany the practice.

Meditation is great, but the real impact we can have is much greater. I have told you that my goal in life is to make people happy. To try to spread genuine happiness to every person I interact with. This is something that came out of my meditation practice. I decided one day that I wanted to use meditation for more than just me, I wanted to use to help others. I wanted to use this new understating of myself and this greater sense of joy and contentment with my life in order to effect change on a larger scale. That is why I started teaching my friends, why I created a community of meditators; and it is even the reason why I wrote this book.

So, you see, meditation is more than just the practice of sitting. It is so much bigger than that. So, make it yours, make it special, and use it to change the world. I know that you can do it and I hope that you will.

**

What advice do you what to give yourself in this moment, right now?

Now go out and live it.

# ACKNOWLEDGMENT:

———

I want to thank all the people who have aided me on my journey. My parents, my brother and sister, my family, my friends. Every person who has influenced me, spoken with me, changed me, to all of these people I thank you. I thank you for helping make me into the person I am today. Without all of you, I wouldn't have been here today, I wouldn't have found meditation, and I wouldn't have been able to write this book.

Over the course of this journey, I also had the pleasure of interviewing some pretty incredible people. I want to acknowledge and thank all of these special people for sharing their stories.

**Dr. Home H.C. Nguyen** (CEO, Executive Coaching & Mindful Leadership Facilitation at MindKind Institute)

**Tara Healy** (Program Director Mindfulness Based Learning at Harvard Pilgrim Health Care)

**Mariann Johnson** (Mindfulness Facilitator and Implementation Manager at Moment Health, United Health Group)

**Lodro Rinzler** (Author of *The Buddha Walks into a Bar*, co-Founder of MNDFL)

**Janice Marturano** (Founder and Executive Director at The Institute for Mindful Leadership)

**Greg Robison** (Executive Director at The Meditatio Foundation)

**Tony Mazurkiewicz** (Director of the John Main Meditation Centre at Georgetown University)

**Yael Shy** (Author of *Why Now? Meditation for your Twenties and Beyond*, Senior Director of Spiritual Life at New York University)

**Graham Betchart** (Author of *Play Present: A Mental Skills Guide for Basketball Players*)

**Sharon Salzberg** (Author, Meditation Teacher and Co-Founder of Insight Meditation Society)

**Jessica Morey** (Executive Director at Inward Bound Mindfulness Education)

**Dr. Judson Brewer** (Author of *The Craving Mind,* Director of Research and Innovation at the Mindfulness Center at Brown University)

**Cory Muscara** (Mindfulness Speaker, Coach and Teacher)

**Brahmachari Sharan** (Director for Hindu Life at Georgetown University)

**Marci Hermann** (Senior Trainer and Consultant at Potential Project – Focused Minds, Organizational Excellence)

My journey has just begun and I cannot wait to see where this world takes me. I cannot wait to thank more people for all of the impact we can have on one another. We can and will change the world, together.

# APPENDIX

---

**INTRODUCTION**

Baker, K. 2014. "How Colleges Flunk Mental Health." *Newsweek. https://www.newsweek.com/2014/02/14/how-colleges-flunk-mental-health-245492.html.*

Holmes, L. 2015. "19 Numbers That Prove We Can Do More For Mental Health". *Huffpost UK.* https://www.huffpost.com/entry/mental-illness-statistics_n_6193660.

"Mental Health and College Students." *Anxiety and Depression Association of America. https://adaa.org/finding-help/helping-others/college-students/facts.*

Novotney, A. 2014. "Students under pressure: College and university counseling centers are examining how best to serve the growing number of students seeking their services". *American Psychological Association. https://www.apa.org/monitor/2014/09/cover-pressure.aspx.*

Reilly, K. 2018. "Record Numbers Of College Students Are Seeking Treatment For Depression And Anxiety — But Schools Can't Keep Up". *Time.* http://time.com/5190291/anxiety-depression-college-university-students/.

"Suicide". 2018. *National Institute Of Mental Health.* https://www.nimh.nih.gov/health/statistics/suicide.shtml.

**MAPPING YOUR JOURNEY**

Frankel, V. 2014. *Man's Search for Meaning.* 6th ed. Boston: Beacon Press.

## PART I: SETTING THE SCENE

### CHAPTER 1
**THE CURSE OF THE MEDITATION GENERATION**

Harris, D. 2016. *#1 Dalai Lama.* 10% Happier.

Harris, D. 2018. *#119 Yael Shy: Helping College Students Fight Stress and FOMO.* 10% Happier.

Shy, Y. 2017. *What Now?: Meditation for your Twenties and Beyond.* California: Parallax Press.

The Dalai Lama, His Holiness and Howard Cutler. 1998. *The Art of Happiness: A Handbook for Living.* New York: Riverhead Books.

## CHAPTER 2

### WHAT IS MEDITATION ANYWAY?

Barch, T. 2018. *FAQ for Meditation – Tara Brach.* Tara Brach. https://www.tarabrach.com/faq-for-meditation2/.

Puddicombe, Andy. *All it takes is 10 mindful minutes.* Filmed November 2012 in London. TEDSalon, 9:18.

## CHAPTER 3

### JUGGLING YOUR MIND

Puddicombe, Andy. *All it takes is 10 mindful minutes.* Filmed November 2012 in London. TEDSalon, 9:18.

The Office of His Holiness the Dalai Lama 2018. *Routine Day.* The 14th Dalai Lama. https://www.dalailama.com/the-dalai-lama/biography-and-daily-life/a-routine-day.

## CHAPTER 4

### THE SCIENCE OF MEDITATION

Blackburn Ph.D., Elizabeth, Elissa Epel Ph.D., Jennifer Daubenmier Ph.D., Judith T. Moskowitz Ph.D. and Susan Folkman Ph.D. "Can meditation slow rate of cellular aging? Cognitive stress, mindfulness, and telomeres." *US National Library of Medicine.* https://www.ncbi.nlm.nih.gov/pmc/articles/PMC3057175/.

Brewer, J. *A simple way to break a habit.* Filmed November 2015. TEDMed, 9:25.

Goyal, MD, Madhav, Sonal Singh, MD, and Eric Sibinga, MD. 2014. "Meditation Programs For Psychological Stress And Well-Being". *JAMA Internal Medicine.* https://jamanetwork.com/journals/jamainternalmedicine/fullarticle/1809754.

Lazar, Ph.D., S. 2018. "The Lazar Lab". *Scholar Harvard.* https://scholar.harvard.edu/sara_lazar/home.

Lazar, S. *How Meditation Can Reshape Our Brains.* Filmed January 2012 in Cambridge, London. TEDxCambridge, 8:33.

Mochel, D. *What are you practicing right now?* Filmed November 2016 in California. TEDxPasadenaWomen, 16:51.


**CHAPTER 5**

**MOTIVATION TOWARD FAILURE**

Harris, D. 2017. #78 *Lodro Rinzler: Meditation for the Heartbroken.* 10% Happier.

The Dalai Lama, His Holiness and Howard Cutler. 1998. *The Art of Happiness: A Handbook for Living.* New York: Riverhead Books.


**PART II: LEARNING A LOT**


**CHAPTER 6**

**STARTING FROM SCRATCH, BUILDING A PRACTICE**

Barch, T. 2018. *FAQ for Meditation – Tara Brach.* Tara Brach. https://www.tarabrach.com/faq-for-meditation2/.

Coelho, P. 1998. *The Pilgrimage.* New York: HarperCollins.

Harris, D. 2017. #60 *Matthieu Ricard: French Born Monk and 'World's Happiest Man'.* 10% Happier.

Harris, D. 2017. #75 *Jon Kabat-Zinn: Creator of Mindfulness Based Stress Reduction*. 10% Happier.

Ricard, M. *The habits of happiness*. Filmed February 2004. TED2004, 20:51.

Tan, C. 2012. *Search Inside Yourself: The Unexpected Path to Achieving Success, Happiness (and World Peace)*. HarperOne.

## CHAPTER 7

### GOING BEYOND THE BASICS

Harris, D. 2016. #8 *Sharon Salzberg*. 10% Happier.

Harris, D. 2017. #78 *Lodro Rinzler: Meditation for the Heartbroken*. 10% Happier.

Millman, D. 2000. *Way of the Peaceful Warrior*. 20th Anniversary Ed. New World Library.

## CHAPTER 8

### ADDING TOOLS TO THE TOOLKIT

"Fact Sheets – Binge Drinking". 2018. *Centers For Disease Control And Prevention*. https://www.cdc.gov/alcohol/fact-sheets/binge-drinking.htm.

Rinzler, L. 2012. *The Buddha Walks into a Bar...A Guide to Life for a Future Generation*. Boston, London: Shambhala.

Tan, C. 2012. *Search Inside Yourself: The Unexpected Path to Achieving Success, Happiness (and World Peace)*. HarperOne.

Tan, Chade-Meng. *Everyday compassion at Google*. Filmed November 2010. TEDPrize@UN, 14:02.

The Mayo Clinic. 2016. "Red wine and resveratrol: Good for your heart?" *The Mayo Clinic. https://www.mayoclinic.org/diseases-conditions/heart-disease/in-depth/red-wine/art-20048281*.

"What Are Eating Disorders?". 2018. *National Eating Disorders Association*. https://www.nationaleatingdisorders.org/what-are-eating-disorders.

**PART III: THE ROLE MEDITATORS**

**CHAPTER 9**

**FINDING FLOW, MEDITATION IN SPORTS**

Harris, D. 2016. *#7 George Mumford*. 10% Happier.

"Kobe Bryant Amazing Last 3 Minutes In His FINAL GAME Vs Jazz (2016.04.13)". 2016. *Youtube*. https://www.youtube.com/watch?v=y64OsZNYhpo.

"Kobe Bryant On Oprah. Meditation Dictates My Day". 2015. *Youtube.* https://www.youtube.com/watch?v=ucNODrsGdxo.

**CHAPTER 10**

**FINDING VALUE, MEDITATION IN BUSINESS**

"About Dr. Richard Davidson". 2018. *Richard J. Davidson.* https://www.richardjdavidson.com/about/.

Harris, D. 2018. #130 *Janice Marturano: How to Be a Better Boss.* 10% Happier.

Institute for Mindful Leadership. 2018. *Home – Institute for Mindful Leadership.* https://instituteformindfulleadership.org/.

John Main Centre for Meditation. 2012. "Ray Dalio On Meditation". *Vimeo.* https://vimeo.com/50999847.

Nemo, J. 2014. "What A NASA Janitor Can Teach Us About Living A Bigger Life". *The Business Journals.* https://www.bizjournals.com/bizjournals/how-to/growth-strategies/2014/12/what-a-nasa-janitor-can-teach-us.html.

Tan, C. 2012. *Search Inside Yourself: The Unexpected Path to Achieving Success, Happiness (and World Peace).* HarperOne.

Tan, Chade-Meng. *Everyday compassion at Google.* Filmed November 2010. TEDPrize@UN, 14:02.

"Understanding The Signals: How Bridgewater Navigated The 2008 Financial Crisis". 2018. *Youtube.* https://www.youtube.com/watch?v=g4LZsG6wo-o&ab_channel=BridgewaterAssociates.

## CHAPTER 11

### FINDING PROOF, MEDITATION AND SCIENCE

Blackburn Ph.D., Elizabeth, Elissa Epel Ph.D., Jennifer Daubenmier Ph.D., Judith T. Moskowitz Ph.D. and Susan Folkman Ph.D. "Can meditation slow rate of cellular aging? Cognitive stress, mindfulness, and telomeres." *US National Library of Medicine.* https://www.ncbi.nlm.nih.gov/pmc/articles/PMC3057175/.

Brewer, J. *A simple way to break a habit.* Filmed November 2015. TEDMed, 9:25.

Golden, Philippe and James Gross. 2014. "Effects of Mindfulness-Based Stress Reduction (MBSR) on Emotion Regulation in Social Anxiety Disorder." *US National Library of Medicine.* https://www.ncbi.nlm.nih.gov/pmc/articles/PMC4203918/.

Harris, D. 2016. #29 *Richard Davidson.* 10% Happier.

Harris, D. 2017. #75 *Jon Kabat-Zinn: Creator of Mindfulness Based Stress Reduction*. 10% Happier.

"History Of MBSR". 2018. *University Of Massachusetts Medical School.* https://www.umassmed.edu/cfm/mindfulness-based-programs/mbsr-courses/about-mbsr/history-of-mbsr/.

Hof, W. 2018. *The History Of The 'Iceman' Wim Hof.* Wim Hof Method. https://www.wimhofmethod.com/iceman-wim-hof.

"Judson Brewer MD Phd – Mindfulness Researcher & "Craving Mind" Author". 2018. *Judson Brewer MD Phd.* https://www.judsonbrewer.com/.

Legg, Tim, Ann Pietrangelo, and Kristen Cherney. 2017. "The Effects Of Depression In Your Body". *Healthline.* https://www.healthline.com/health/depression/effects-on-body#1.

"Mission – Mind & Life Institute". 2018. *Mind & Life Institute.* Accessed October 7. https://www.mindandlife.org/mission/.

## CHAPTER 12

## FINDING BALANCE, MEDITATING THROUGH LIFE'S UPS AND DOWNS

Harris, D. 2016. #8 *Sharon Salzberg*. 10% Happier.

Harris, D. 2018. #119 *Yael Shy: Helping College Students Fight Stress and FOMO.* 10% Happier.

"Home". 2018. *Phakyab Rinpoche.* https://www.phakyabrinpoche.org/index.php/en/.

"Mental Health and College Students." *Anxiety and Depression Association of America.* https://adaa.org/finding-help/helping-others/college-students/facts.

Shy, Y. 2017. *What Now?: Meditation for your Twenties and Beyond.* California: Parallax Press.

## PART IV: LET'S DO THIS, JUMP-STARTING YOUR JOURNEY

### CHAPTER 13
#### MEDITATION FOR ATHLETES

Betchart, G. 2015. *Play Present: A Mental Skills Training Program for Basketball Players.*

### CHAPTER 14
#### MINDFUL LEADERSHIP

Harris, D. 2018. #130 *Janice Marturano: How to Be a Better Boss.* 10% Happier.

Institute for Mindful Leadership. 2018. *Home – Institute for Mindful Leadership.* https://instituteformindfulleadership.org/.

Mautz, S. 2017. "Psychology And Neuroscience Blow-Up The Myth Of Effective Multitasking". *Inc.* https://www.inc.com/scott-mautz/psychology-and-neuroscience-blow-up-the-myth-of-effective-multitasking.html.

**CHAPTER 15**

**THE SKEPTICAL GURU**

Harris, D. 2016. *#29 Richard Davidson.* 10% Happier.

Tan, C. 2012. *Search Inside Yourself: The Unexpected Path to Achieving Success, Happiness (and World Peace).* HarperOne.

**CHAPTER 16**

**STRUGGLING MINDFULLY**

Barch, T. 2018. *FAQ for Meditation – Tara Brach.* Tara Brach. https://www.tarabrach.com/faq-for-meditation2/.

Harris, D. 2016. *#8 Sharon Salzberg.* 10% Happier.

Harris, D. 2018. *#119 Yael Shy: Helping College Students Fight Stress and FOMO.* 10% Happier.

Shy, Y. 2017. *What Now?: Meditation for your Twenties and Beyond.* California: Parallax Press.


## CHAPTER 17

### AVERAGE JOE, TURNED MEDITATION EXPERT

"Breaking The Sugar Habit – An Inspirational Story Attributed To Gandhi". 2018. *Habitsforwellbeing.Com.* https://www.habitsforwellbeing.com/breaking-the-sugar-habit-an-inspirational-story-attributed-to-gandhi/.


Harris, D. 2017. *#82 Cory Muscara: Mindfulness Teacher, Former Monk.* 10% Happier.


Millman, D. 2000. *Way of the Peaceful Warrior.* 20th Anniversary Ed. New World Library.